the green book

Also by Amitava Kumar

The Blue Book: A Writer's Journal

The Yellow Book: A Traveller's Diary

the green book
an observer's notebook

amitava kumar

HarperCollins *Publishers* India

First published in India by HarperCollins *Publishers* 2024
4th Floor, Tower A, Building No. 10, Phase II, DLF Cyber City,
Gurugram, Haryana – 122002
www.harpercollins.co.in

2 4 6 8 10 9 7 5 3 1

P-ISBN: 978-93-6569-275-4
E-ISBN: 978-93-6569-919-7

Cover and inside design: Gavin Morris

Printed and bound at
Nutech Print Services - India

Baby peach tree, Poughkeepsie, 2024

For Ila and Rahul

And for Cade, Evie, Felix,
Levi, Matilda, Saya and Zeke

Virginia Woolf's green notebook of travels 1906-09, British Library, London, 2022

And all the lives we ever lived and all the lives
to be are full of trees and changing leaves.
— Virginia Woolf

Contents

Introduction

I am writing these words in the New York Public Library where I have been working as a Cullman Center Fellow during the academic year 2023-24. During this period, starting in September, I completed work on my latest novel, *My Beloved Life*. Since then, my energies have been devoted to work on the book that you are holding in your hands. From the library, I ventured out on some days to the Central Park, and on other days, upstairs to the archives to look at the journals and drawings of writers like the Brontë sisters, Henry David Thoreau, Vladimir Nabokov, Jack Kerouac and Annie Proulx. I was interested in these writers because I wanted to follow their example: they were known primarily for the words they put on the page but each had also given expression to a different kind of artistic passion. They had made drawings, paintings, collages. These were often mixed genre creations.

One of the earliest encounters with a work of that kind—here in one of the library research rooms on the floor above my Cullman Center office—was with *The New Yorker* writer Janet Malcolm's book of photographs titled *Burdock*. In this book, Malcolm has collected her photographs of the leaves of what is widely regarded in the US merely as a weed, the burdock plant. A photograph of a leaf looking like a tattered flag with holes, a leaf limned with dry brown parts, a green leaf with small specks of discolouration, another with a cobweb of what must be some kind of disease, and in yet another, white marks crawling over the leaf's surface like caterpillars (or maybe they *were* caterpillars). Such curiosity about what I'm tempted to call small ravaged landscapes hiding the mystery of life and inevitable death.

Burdock, Homage to Janet Malcom, New York, 2024

In the text accompanying the photographs in the book I came across an observation by Malcolm that is a profound acknowledgement of art's ability to lend significance: 'In the case of my aged and diseased leaves, the camera exercises another of its transformative capacities: it confers aesthetic value on the apparently plain and worthless.' Is it really the camera though? I believe it is the person behind the camera, Malcolm herself, who is the agent of that transformation of the mundane into something remarkable. Malcolm is being self-effacing but the general point is indisputable: attention paid by the artist saves objects (and arguably, people) from the world's indifference. That is perhaps the point of noticing, of observing. The painting above is one I did in oil on a wood panel. It pays homage to what Malcolm accomplished in *Burdock* and what she offered as a credo for our conduct on this earth: 'Looking at natural forms close up is an exercise in awe. The botanical illustrators never failed to convey their sense of the mystery that adheres to the gorgeousness of the particulars of the things that are alive in this world.'

The last of the snowdrops, Poughkeepsie, 2024

Trees

Yellowwood tree, Poughkeepsie, 2023

'Even if I knew that tomorrow the world would go to pieces, I would still plant my apple tree,' said Martin Luther. 'On the last day of the world I would want to plant a tree,' wrote W.S. Merwin. And Louise Erdrich has this sage advice: 'When it happens that you are broken, or betrayed, or left, or hurt, or death brushes near, let yourself sit by an apple tree and listen to the apples falling all around you in heaps, wasting their sweetness. Tell yourself you tasted as many as you could.'

In February 2023, exactly a month before my father died, I noted down the following quote from May Sarton in my journal: 'Keep busy with survival. Imitate the trees. Learn to lose in order to recover, and remember that nothing stays the same for long, not even pain, psychic pain. Sit it out. Let it all pass.'

In the Indian subcontinent, our literature has built an affective tradition around trees. They are distinct characters and represent a link to feelings of home. Perhaps because trees, unlike humans, possess roots. One of the best examples of this representation occurs in Intizar Husain's novel *Basti*. Zakir is Husain's protagonist, a historian, who has migrated from India to Pakistan. In his newly adopted homeland he misses the trees of his past. He asks a friend, 'Aren't there any neem trees here?' He is taken to a park and soon they are standing under what he is told is a neem tree. Zakir says, 'Yaar, this is Persian lilac.'

His friend is embarrassed and assures him that they can search for a neem tree. Zakir is pierced by a yearning for the home he has lost. 'But we never had to search for neem trees!

In the afternoons when the desert wind blew, and in the rainy July days, their greenness always proclaimed their presence.'

जिए तो अपने घर में गुलमोहर के तले,
मरे तो गैर की गलियों में गुलमोहर के लिए

In my teens, ever since I first read the above two lines from the poet Dushyant Kumar, I have always thought of the gulmohur with particular affection. (Such is the power of words! And of literature!) How are we to translate those words?

Let life find me in my own garden
Under the flowers of the gulmohur
Or if death is to ambush me, let it be in the streets of strangers
In search of the gulmohur

In his novel *The Overstory*, Richard Powers provides an introduction to what we might call the inner life of trees. 'We found that trees could communicate, over the air and through their roots,' a scientist explains in *The Overstory*. 'That trees feed their young and synchronize their masts and bank resources and warn kin and send out signals to wasps to come and save them from attacks.' In an interview, Powers described his novel as an experiment in attempting 'to grant personhood, to grant character status, to grant subjectivity to the non-human.' This emotion would be recognizable to our own poets and writers. But Powers is also making a further argument. He has said: 'The history of civilization can in some ways be seen as the gradual expansion of who gets to be a person. … We grant personhood to companies … so why shouldn't we be able to bring out a lawsuit on behalf of a river

Gulmohur, 2024

or a mountain or an ecosystem or a stand of trees?' When put in this way, we are not talking of trees as motif of romance or mere nostalgia. Rather, to make this leap is to face the crisis of the anthropocene where the dominance of the human, his arrogance as much as his greed, has brought the planet to the brink of annihilation.

Outside my study, Poughkeepsie, 2023

When I look outside the window in my study, I see the yellowwood tree in my backyard. I have sketched and painted it many times, particularly its white flowers that always draw out gasps of admiration from my wife, Mona, who is in the habit of declaring that this yellowwood is her favourite tree. As a way of showing my love for her, I paint that tree again and again in different seasons. Several years ago, when my daughter was very young, she had a pet hamster. When he or she died, I buried him or her under the yellowwood. The tree would always give shade to the hamster.

Last winter, we discovered that the trees on the far side of our backyard, beyond the yellowwood that stands in the middle, had been cut down. I made a painting of the chopped trees and wrote a poem describing what had happened. Which is all to say, I was once again trying to communicate with my wife. I wrote the poem first in Hindi—ah, the pleasure of using one's own mother tongue in a foreign land—and then I translated it into English.

बर्फ गिरने से पहले

आज सुबह पत्नी ने कहा
की सेंट्रल हडसन बिजली कंपनी ने
बिना बताये
तीन पेड़ काट दिए
हमारे घर के पिछवाड़े में

एक लेख लिख रहा था मैं
एक कलाकार के बारे में जिसने

बचपन में देखा था अपनी माँ को
अपना ही चेहरा काटते हुए
परिवार के सारे फोटो से

झाँक के बाहर देखा खिड़की के
और फिर अपनी पत्नी को
जीना कितना सरल हो जाता
कुछ कहना हो जाता
इतना ही आसान

Before the Storm

This morning my wife said to me
that the Central Hudson electric company
without telling us
had cut down three trees
in our backyard.

I was writing an essay
about an artist who had seen,
as a child, her mother
cutting out her own face
from all the family photographs.

I looked out of the window
and then at my wife.
How easy
would living become
if it was easy to say anything.

Central Hudson, 2023

Fall, Poughkeepsie, 2023

Fall, Poughkeepsie, 2023

Snow, 2023

Snow, 2023

In 2021, the artist Maya Lin installed a sculpture in Madison Square Park, a 'ghost forest' of forty-nine dying Atlantic white cedar trees. The purpose of this public project was to call attention to the fact that 'climate change is causing vast tracts of forested lands to die off'. These trees used by Lin were sourced from the Pine Barrens of New Jersey—saltwater from Hurricane Sandy had caused the cedars to slowly die—where these trees have been reduced to under 10 per cent of their original habitat. In her statement, Lin wrote: 'We have very little time left to alter our climate change emission patterns and our way of living within the natural world. I wanted to bring awareness to a die-off that is happening all over the world.' Lin's artistic practice represents for me the greening of the art gallery. Not just climatologists and scientists, everyone has a role to play in the rescue of our world, and Lin's visionary installation was a remarkable exercise of a critical imagination.

I read the words from Maya Lin that I have cited above in a book titled *The Language of Trees* that was put together by the artist Katie Holten. Holten's own contribution to the book is a new font, a typeface made of trees, where each alphabet of the English alphabet is replaced by a tree. The letter 'A' is a drawing of an apple tree, the letter 'L' is a drawing of a linden, the letter 'W' is a drawing of a weeping willow. Holten calls this font that she has created 'a rewilding too'.

Another essay in the book, this one by Gaia Vince, introduces readers to a scientist named Klaus Lackner who has designed 'an artificial tree that soaks up carbon dioxide from the air using "leaves" that are 1,000 times more efficient than natural leaves.' Vince explains that Lackner's leaves 'look like sheets of papery plastic and are coated in a resin which pulls carbon dioxide out of the air and stores it as a bicarbonate (baking soda) on the leaf. To remove the carbon dioxide, the leaves are rinsed in water vapour and can dry naturally in the wind, soaking up more carbon dioxide.' According to Lackner, his tree can remove one ton of carbon dioxide a day. This sounded like good news to me, the fact that vast artificial forests might yet save the planet. But at the end of the report, Vince asks an urgent question: 'How fickle will our care for forests be, once we discover artificial replacements ...?'

Joyce Kilmer, the poet who met his death as a soldier during the First World War, had written: 'I think that I shall never see / A poem lovely as a tree.' The sad truth is that unless we place trees and plants and the green grass at the heart of our scientific and creative imaginations, the world that we know will no longer be habitable and life will be doomed, possibly eternally.

Overleaf:
Maya Lin,
2023

Ever since I was a child I have watched lovers in Hindi films running around trees, looking a bit silly, professing (or pretending to hide) their love. I like better those sequences in films where young women sit on swings that hang from the branches of trees. A different rhythm, put to great use in inventive ways by auteurs like Satyajit Ray, Rituparno Ghosh, Shyam Benegal. I have this memory from a film I had watched in my youth, *Junoon*. The rains have come. Desire has been released into the air, and also rivalries in love. A young woman pushes the swing on which sits her friend and future rival while a singer in the background goes on about the monsoon with a lyrical, piercing pathos. All such songs are about love even when they are not about love. I have tried to draw or paint the yellowwood, which I think of now as my wife's tree, in different seasons.

For a few short years when I was an undergraduate in Delhi, I lived near Lodhi Gardens and went there often on long walks. On some days I returned to draw a semul tree I liked. There was also a giant semul in front of the apartment where I lived in Delhi; now, decades later, whenever I pass that area in a taxi, I still look for that tree. Recently, when writing my novel *My Beloved Life*, I put in its pages the banyan tree that has remained rooted beside a pond in the earth of my ancestral village. It has been there all my life, and I hope it lasts long after I am gone. That banyan tree in my village and also the rosewood trees that I had known only by the Hindi name sheesham will continue to stand also in my book. In the opening pages of my novel *Immigrant, Montana*, we read the following line: 'The red-bottomed monkeys of my childhood would leave the branches of the big tamarind tree and peel the oranges left unattended on the balcony of Lotan Mamaji's house.' That book was a work of fiction, of course, but that big tamarind tree was real.

Two paintings in Saratoga One Studio, Yaddo, 2023

In his famous story 'Funes the Memorius', Jorge Luis Borges writes: 'Funes not only remembered every leaf on every tree of every wood, but even every one of the times he had perceived or imagined it.' I do not, alas, have the ability that Funes possessed but various trees stand in my memory, like the ones during the summer of 2023, that I would see each day outside my studio at Yaddo. When I was painting those trees—on two wood panels at the same time—I was trying to fix them in my memory. But many of these remembered trees stretch back into the distant years of my childhood, including the tree made immortal, even in death, in Gieve Patel's poem 'On Killing a Tree'. It is a poem that is familiar to many Indians from their English textbooks in middle or high school. When I had read it at school in Patna several decades ago I had accepted the poem as a story about the ways in which one must work hard and persevere to complete a given task. The shift that has taken place in ecological thinking but also my own maturity is now responsible for a different reading of the poem. It is impossible to read 'On Killing a Tree' today without thinking of nature's resilience, the enormous fight put up by life-giving trees in their struggle against the depredations of the human race.

A tree that I have drawn only once or twice during these past few years when I have been making art is an American beech. It is not visible from my study and I haven't ever sat contemplating it from any other window. But on New Year's Day this year, while driving home to America from Canada, I was listening to the 'Empire' podcast and I heard a haunting description that connected a falling leaf to a meditation on life and death. The podcast episode was on Lawrence of Arabia.

The guest on the podcast, an historian, said that the line about the falling leaf had been written by T.E. Lawrence before his death. Even as I heard the historian's words, I saw very clearly in my mind the dried leaves of the American beech that I find each autumn in my parking space. When I reached home, I got out of the car and picked up one of those leaves and then, arriving in my study, I searched online for the words written by the dying Lawrence near the end of his short life in a letter to a friend. Here they are: 'You wonder what I am doing? Well, so do I, in truth. Days seem to dawn, suns to shine, evenings to follow, and then I sleep. What have I done, what am I going to do, puzzle and bewilder me. Have you ever been a leaf and fallen from your tree in autumn and been really puzzled about it? That's the feeling.'

Before going on sleep on that first night of the year, I made a collage using my American beech leaf and recycled cardboard and newsprint.

Overleaf:
Falling leaf
(American beech),
2024

My drawing of John Berger's notebook, its green cover partially discoloured, in the manuscripts section of the British Library, 2022

On Notebooks

In the archives and manuscripts section of the British Library in London, there is a small notebook. It is 4x6 inches in size, with a black-and-white print on the cover that says 'The Iveagh Bequest, Kenwood'.

The first entry in the notebook begins: 'Nov. 1st. And so, suddenly, I'm off to India. The last time I had gone it was because of another death—that of Sanjay.'

No Photography Allowed: A drawing of Shiva Naipaul's notebook stored in the British Library. Researchers are not permitted to photograph a lot of the material preserved in the archives and manuscripts section.

This notebook belonged to the writer Shiva Naipaul. It has only twenty-eight pages filled with minute, cramped handwriting, while the rest of the pages remain blank. In those few pages, Naipaul made his notes when he flew to India to report on the days that followed Prime Minister Indira Gandhi's assassination on 31 October 1984.

I am interested in writers' notebooks. They provide a record of thinking.

If the writer is travelling, you are also able to witness him or her in the act of looking. There is something else that is fascinating about such notebooks. You want to see what made it into the printed copy.

First you have the changes or even corrections made in the hastily-written-down account, and then, perhaps more significantly, it is possible to see the further transformation when you compare what is recorded in the notebook with what appears in published form. All writing is only rewriting. The traveller's notebook provides evidence of quick, fertile observations and, at the same time, an insight into the process of revision.

It is clear from the first page of Shiva Naipaul's 1984 notebook that he wrote the first words while he was en route to India. During a stop-over, in 'the cream-coloured halls of Kuwait airport', he asks an Australian journalist how long he planned to stay in India. The Australian responds, 'How long will it take for them to stop killing each other?' From other conversations on the plane, Naipaul reports: 'All the way, rumours of riot, of civil disobedience.' To me, these notes reveal the early eagerness at the start of the journey. The writer wants to absorb everything being discussed around him. He is preparing himself for the real task that lies ahead.

I also detect a certain nervousness.

Like an actor who might look at the mirror in the green room and practice his expressions before stepping on stage, Naipaul is trying to slip into the character of the writer he must become in order to get the job done. While still on the plane, he writes in the notebook that 'Mrs. G. was the victim of communalism—the curse of India...' And then goes on: 'India divides, breaks up each and every way. So, what is the "India" we talk about? Does it exist? *Should* it exist? Has it *earned* the right to exist?' Those two words, underlined by Naipaul for added emphasis, strike me as presumptuous and certainly naïve. These are the thoughts of a man 12,000 metres in the air with no real feel for the power of the nation-state or the undeniable fact of a large, if unwieldy, polity.

I was more drawn to Naipaul's concrete observations. Here is the next entry, which he has made upon arrival: 'Delhi in the dawn, smelling of smoke, hazy on the road in from the airport... On a roundabout, a burnt-out bus, the smoking remains of a lorry.'

When I read those lines, I stopped. I asked the librarian at the British Library to find for me the newspaper-piece which Naipaul had published under the title 'The Death of Indira Gandhi'. This is the final form that these notes had taken: 'The still smouldering wreck of an overturned lorry was abandoned on a grassy roundabout. A calm of sorts had descended after a night of riot and pillage and murder. But it was an eerie dawn. Delhi had become a city of rumor and dread.'

In the above lines, the initial observations have been given a better syntactic structure and rhythm. The simple use of the word 'rioting' in the notes has been replaced by the more informed and emphatic phrase: 'a night of riot and pillage and murder'. (In the printed text there is the beauty of repetition: 'burnt-out buses, burnt-out taxis'.) The mention of the 'roundabout' has been moved to the end of the sentence and the adjective 'grassy' added for effect. These are instructive improvements.

In Naipaul's notes I had liked the sentence 'A sad, stunned city.' But I didn't find it in the final version. I had been attracted by the alliteration, which in that short sentence sounded to my ear like a bell tolling. Why did Naipaul or his editor choose to cut it out? I speculated that Naipaul had seen the deserted streets on his drive from the airport and noted down that phrase but upon learning more about the massacre of the Sikhs he had rightly chosen to highlight the murder and mayhem instead of the grief.

I was sitting in a library in London reading descriptions of a city where I had been living as a student when the events described had taken place. The words I was reading excited a great curiosity in me because there was this writer, older than I was at that time, who was writing about what he saw in Delhi and its streets even as Mrs Gandhi was lying in state in Teen Murti.

I had also liked this observation in the notebook: 'Mainly men, a sense, I feel of suppressed violence rather than of suppressed grief.' What had made him write this? I cannot know but they intrigue me. These words didn't make it to the finished piece—perhaps the editor decided that there wasn't anything concretely verifiable.

Another observation I found remarkable, this one from the cremation. Was Naipaul sitting in his hotel room watching television, sipping on a drink, writing down quickly what he so quickly judged? It wasn't in the published piece either, perhaps because Naipaul had not been present on the scene—but I liked reading it, not least because it had the familiar irascibility displayed by the writer's elder brother: 'The familiar confusion of the Indian ceremonial—the gestures, the undisciplined movements, the lack of perceived pattern, the gracelessness, in a way—casual stepping over the sandalwood, the unorchestrated moments... The tins of ghee—no vessels of beauty. Strange in a ritual of death so ancient.' The writing here was so bitter, and so deeply felt, that my memory suddenly conjured, with no fealty to reality, the tins of Dalda sitting awkwardly on the ground near where Rajiv Gandhi was circling the pyre.

At the very end, on the last two pages of the notebook, Naipaul had neatly written down in brisk, skeletal phrases the order in which he was going to broach the topics. He followed this structural arrangement to a great extent, especially the repeated switch from descriptions of what he saw in Delhi to a recounting of political history. I liked the rigour or the discipline of this practice. It helps to diagram a piece before you write. But why place it at the very end? I was puzzled by all the sixty blank pages in between. What had he wanted to write there? The notebook takes you closer to the writer but then—no further.

I once saw a curator's note at the entrance of the 'Treasures' room at the British Library: 'To see a first draft in the hand of the author can have a powerful effect on the viewer. The hasty scrawl that reveals a moment of inspiration, or the violent crossing out that signifies a change of mind, are part of what of what poet Philip Larkin termed the "magical quality of manuscripts".'

My immediate recognition of the truth of that sentiment was based in my own recent experience. For the past several days before I saw that note, I had been visiting the British Library to look at authors' notebooks. I have mentioned one of Shiva Naipaul's notebooks above. Another of his notebooks in the manuscripts section contained Naipaul's notes on another visit to India and also to Liverpool in 1978. When he was in India, Naipaul wrote on a single page a much-revised 'letter to the editor'. I have no idea whether it was published or not. 'I was "shocked and saddened" by the small article about me which was printed in your newspaper. The relationship between what was said there and what I actually told your reporter was quite tenuous.' Some of the distortions were trivial and others were gross. Among the lines Naipaul had scratched out was this one: 'Never again will I speak to anyone associated with your newspaper.' I could understand the reasons behind this deletion, but I felt the following lines, also deleted, ought to have been restored: 'Your journalists should be taught not only how to write but how to tell the truth. The truth, curiously enough, can be quite interesting.' I had liked the simple truth-telling of the deleted lines. I also liked that Naipaul had fussed over what he was writing. All the deletions, particularly toward the end, made me suspect that he had run out of steam. Or simply that he was satisfied that he had at least expressed his outrage on the page. He had written it out for himself, perhaps sitting in his hotel room, and it was enough. These are, of course, speculations on my part. But perhaps because I too have found the methods of some journalists that I have met rather appalling—this last word was also among those deleted in Naipaul's letter—I would have liked to see the notebook entry in print. In bringing them to light here, I'm trying to bring that act to its conclusion.

In another notebook, a black rectangular one this time, I came across notes that Shiva Naipaul had made during a different visit to India. This one was from 1973. I read and wrote down his observations from different cities. Then, a gap of several days in the notes. 22 January to 8 February. The 8 February entry begins: 'After a long, lazy lapse have decided to keep this diary as up to date as possible. It is such a pity to let separate impressions merge and blur.' So far, I had been interested in what, and how, the writer was looking at the places and people he was passing through, but what arrested me here is the observation he makes about writing itself: if you write it down, the moment will retain its particularity. In the absence of such a practice, it is all out of focus, as if you were peering out through a film of tears. *It is such a pity to let separate impressions merge and blur.*

Penelope Fitzgerald's notebook in the British library.
I made this drawing in April 2022.

I had read Penelope Fitzgerald's novel *The Beginning of Spring* and found it fine and mysterious; furthermore, I had wondered how she knew small details about Moscow and life there during the years before the First World War. Then, in the British Library, I found her slim red memo book. Fitzgerald had written down the earlier title for the novel

(The Greenhouse) and, in blue ink surrounded by water stains, revealed the first outline of the proposed book: 'Harry's wife leaves him, taking children (one boy 2 girls) with her. In letter explaining this she gives some of the reasons, which describe what it's like in Moscow. Include vulgarity of Harry's friends, a Russian merchant, M.' On the pages that follow are signs of the novelist trying to figure out and advance the plot and the story. 'Suddenly children are returned—they're all by themselves at station. Brings them back. Who to look after them? Borrow the governess? ... Masha to have troubling effect on Harry. Builds greenhouse now to take his mind off her.' Also on the same page, in block letters, 'BEAR STORY.' The bear story refers to a wonderful, dramatic incident in which, at the home of the Russian merchant, a baby bear is given vodka to drink. It gets drunk and wants more. Soon, the bear is wreaking havoc, pulling down the tablecloth, breaking bottles, slurping the spilled drinks. It sprays the carpet with urine. Drawn by the shouting and the laughter, a servant comes into the room and snatching a shovel, throws coal from the fire onto the drunk bear. The bear screams, 'its screams like those of a human child'. Fitzgerald's notebook lists the names of books and articles she uses for her research; there are notes on everything from anarchism in Russia to the repair of dachas, from notes on Tolstoy to annotated drawings of the kinds of mushrooms to be found in the countryside.

All this research gets quite subtly absorbed into the narrative, and I find it instructive. However, what the notebooks don't reveal—and this I learned from reading Hermione Lee's excellent biography, *Penelope Fitzgerald: A Life*—are the more specific ways in which the borrowing takes place. Lee informs us that one of the titles I had seen listed in Fitzgerald's notes, the travel guide *Baedeker's Russia 1914*, provides so much of the information that appears in the novel, including its opening line: 'In 1913 the journey from Moscow to Charing Cross, changing at Warsaw, cost fourteen pounds, six shillings and three pence and took two and a half days.' Here's Lee: 'Sure enough, *Baedeker's Russia* for 1914 informs you that the train—going the other way from Charing Cross to Moscow via Warsaw—takes two and a half days and costs £14. 6s. 3d. Baedeker gave her everything she needed by way of maps,

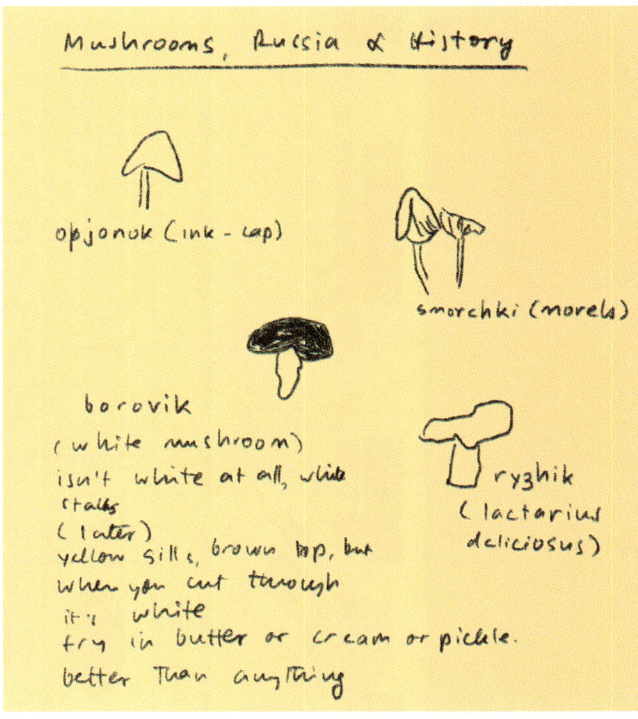

Hand-copied from Penelope Fitzgerald's notebook, 2022

place-names, shops, markets, restaurants, parks, churches, stations, concert halls, passport requirements…' (These lines made me wonder if I had ever made clever and adequate use of Wikipedia.)

The more startling revelation in Lee's book was about the aforementioned bear story. In a book called *The Smiths in Moscow* (1984) by Harvey Pitcher, Fitzgerald had come across a description of a party where a bear had been given vodka. When her novel was coming out, Fitzgerald wrote to Pitcher seeking permission to use that story. Lee writes: 'He was happy to oblige, and a friendly correspondence ensued.' And then Lee slyly goes on: 'He would have noticed many other links, too, between *The Smiths of Moscow* and *The Beginning of Spring*: the English families' dacha outside Moscow, set in woods of silver birches, the corruption and obstructiveness of government and police, the assimilation of the English children, all of whom spoke perfect Russian and felt completely at home in Moscow.' Then, Lee goes on to list other borrowings.

As I begin work on a new book, here's my prayer to my gentle muses: teach me please to maintain a notebook! And please give me the strength and guile to borrow freely and imaginatively.

*

I like to read in a writer's notebooks about their ambitions, their anxieties.

In the middle of February, I had the chance to look at Jack Kerouac's little spiral notebook from 1953. Using a ball-point pen, he had written 'SK 11' on the stiff cover, SK short for 'Sketchings'. The notebook is in the Berg Collection at the New York Public Library. In Kerouac's notebook, apart from his notes, there are drawings of edible as well as poisonous mushrooms, plants, etc. At that time he was making these notes, Kerouac's *On the Road* was still in the future: it would be published four years later. In his sketches here, he is an observer of scenes and even his dreams—and certainly of nature around him. He is also anxious. One entry reads: 'dear God, please making me a writer again'.

At the time that I was reading Kerouac's notebook, I was anxiously awaiting the publication of my novel *My Beloved Life*. A writer friend told me that when he was younger, the novelist Don DeLillo, older and more experienced, had advised him that when you are in this situation, the best thing you can do for your sanity is to be working on a new project. Have the next book mapped out, let it absorb your attention. This was difficult, of course, but that was the reason why I had been spending time with writers' notebooks and their nature drawings. I was working on this book in your hands.

It wasn't easy to focus. I was self-conscious and stood looking, as if through a window, into a room where my real self was seated. I wondered what the reviews of the novel would be like. Would that particular editor at a leading periodical, for instance, send it to X, under the impression that, well, X is Indian and therefore of course is the right person to review. But X might have a history very different from mine and would possibly not be interested in the book at all. In fact, X, anxious about proving his authenticity in this part of the world, might want to impose his sense of reality over mine and might want to scold me for not having written the book he wants me to write. Rather, the book he would himself want to write. *But X has not written a book! No, X hasn't. It makes X very bitter. Or X has written several mediocre books and never received what he thinks is his due. He will get his revenge by killing my book.* When I got caught in the swirl of these thoughts it was my turn to be bitter. I felt myself unable to work on the new project. I had angry thoughts.

And that is where Kerouac came to my rescue. He offered a lesson in how 'to drive out angry thoughts'. In his little notebook, using a pencil, he had written: 'Whatever anyone does, anyone says, in the past, now, everything, let it bounce off the rock of yr gladness...'

The rock of yr gladness! Thank you, Jack.

I saw that in one of his entries in SK11, Kerouac had recorded a visit to an astrologer. He has made drawings of 'Blanche Fortunetelling's cards of me'. She told him that he was 'inwardly disturbed'. (Me too, me too, I cried in the silence of the library.) Back in my youth, when I was unable to get a room in the Delhi University hostel, and nothing else seemed to be going right in the world, an uncle of mine back in the village in Champaran said that I should put a bit of saffron in my navel every day. I hadn't heard of anything stranger than this but I was taken with this suggestion because this uncle of mine, my father's second cousin, had been giving advice also to the chief minister of Bihar at that time, Jagannath Mishra. When I next went for my interview with the hostel administrator, I was careful to do what my uncle had instructed. It didn't help. (I have written about this in my 2002 literary memoir *Bombay-London-New York.*)

Anyway, as I said, I was now nervous about the new novel coming out. Would it find readers? Why should any reader or reviewer agree with this undoubtedly kind-hearted and, most important, wise reviewer in a pre-publication magazine who had written that *My Beloved Life* offered 'an immersive, moving portrait that steadily gathers intensity, vividness, and surprise'? Tastes differ, this is a free country, to each her own, etc.

I asked a loving and close relative of mine in Patna what I should do. She spoke to a priest who said I should make an offering of rice to the needy on a Monday. I bought a bag of rice. It turned out that the Hindu temple was closed till 5 p.m. But there was a food drop-off place at my son's school for a community kitchen. That is where I left the bag of rice.

Postcards from the Ganga

Mountains and a river, en route to Devprayag, 2023

New York. In the taxi to JFK, I checked the weather app. The local temperature in New York was 62 degrees Fahrenheit (that would be just over 18 degrees Celsius). I then checked Delhi's weather. It was night there and the temperature was 97 degrees Fahrenheit, or 35 degrees Celsius. 'Mostly cloudy. Feels like 114 degrees.' The *Hindustan Times* had a headline about Delhi: 'Monsoon could hit city by weekend.' The paper also reported that if the rainclouds reached Mumbai on 26 June instead of a day earlier, this would break the record for the most delayed arrival of the monsoon in this century.

I had bought an expensive raincoat and put my passport and money in a waterproof bag. My plan was to reach Delhi and then take a train to Haridwar where I would hire a taxi north to Devprayag, the place where the stream of Bhagirathi joins the waters of Alaknanda and becomes the Ganga. Then I would visit the various towns and cities on the river's banks until, two thousand kilometres later, the Ganga empties into the sea.

Earlier in the year, in March, my father died. We took his body to Varanasi for the cremation at Manikarnika Ghat. The ritual of cremation followed a routine; I was the karta, the one who with his head shaven and clad only in unstitched clothing, sets alight the funeral pyre. I felt I had to observe the rituals from a distance, customs that seemed obsolete and irrelevant to me, and I often felt divided from my grief.

During this travel down the Ganga, I wanted to return to my father's death in solitude, a solitude that travel confers on you if you are by yourself and discovering places in a new way. Instead of merely going to Varanasi I wanted to begin at the beginning. That was why the journey first to Devprayag.

*

New Delhi. On the plane from New York, I was reading a book by Alexander Frater titled *Chasing the Monsoon*. Fine descriptions of the wall of water that is the Indian monsoon. But Delhi was dry when I arrived. No sign of the monsoon yet. I was told that there had been rain three or four days earlier. The previous week, I had been on a family vacation on Long Island. When sitting in the sauna, I had tried to imagine what it would feel like once I was in Delhi. Nothing now needed to be left to the imagination. When I stepped out of the airconditioned car, my glasses fogged up.

BBC reported the arrest of an Indian man in a five-star Delhi hotel who had checked in for one night but managed to stay two years for free. He now owed the hotel five million rupees or seventy thousand dollars.

*

Haridwar. I boarded the Vande Bharat Express in Delhi for Haridwar. All my life the trains in India had been mostly rust-coloured; this one was painted white and blue and when it entered the station people were filming it on their phones. Even when the train was passing through the countryside, people held their phones up to record this latest mark of our modernity. At one point, from my train window, I saw a crowd gathered around a cow that had been struck by an earlier train. Two logs had been slid under the dark-brown hide and scrawny youth were trying to move the weight under the eyes of policemen who stood stiffly at a distance.

We were passing fields of sugarcane and corn. Shallow plots of paddy with egrets, their white wings folded as if in prayer. The monsoon was necessary for these fields. Once, I also saw a field of marigolds. When the train had started its journey in Delhi, everyone was screaming into their phones, but after an hour the shouting had ceased. On the way to the train station, I had picked up a copy of V.S. Naipaul's *An Area of Darkness*. I had read the book before but there was a surprise for me: in this edition, Naipaul had supplied a new preface. I had always believed that the book had been born out of great distress and disappointment, a kind of reckoning with the ancestral homeland and its deficiencies; but the new preface revealed that the writer had experienced an entirely different kind of anxiety while he was in India: he suffered from the fear that he had run out of fictional material after having written *A House for Mr Biswas*. He was anxious about his place as a writer. He had tried to place a piece or two about India with the English papers but had failed. 'I had no success; I had no reputation.' An editor in London had told him that India was 'inexhaustible' but that they would be happy to take a look at what he came up with. I wondered who would publish what I was going to write about this journey I was about to undertake.

Close to ten at night, the train brought me to Haridwar. I was delivered from the airconditioned train-car into the warm, muggy air. A statue of Shiva painted a shiny blue—the god of destruction looking placid, maybe sad, even mildly stoned—was the central piece outside the station around which sleeping bodies were arrayed. I made my way past the crowd to my hotel and found it after several twists and turns in a dark and narrow alley. Not even my reading of Naipaul's dyspeptic prose had prepared me for the hotel room with its dirty walls. Filth had settled on every piece of furniture. An insect lay dead in one of the two cups sitting next to a thermos flask that I dared not open. The curtain was bunched up and tied with string that I couldn't unknot. The light from the street was very bright. I called the front desk to ask if I could have soap in the bathroom and if someone could help me with the curtain. A boy of maybe thirteen or fourteen came up to do the job. He was unable to untie the knot; helpless, he tugged hard on the twine. It broke free but got caught in the ceiling fan. No damage done other than the fright it caused us when the blade hit the twine. After the youth had left, I saw that the accident with the fan had left small furry bits of dirt from the blade all over the bed.

*

Haridwar. It was still dark outside when I woke up and decided to go to the river. Once in my early twenties I had been brought here, to Har ki Pauri. Here the waters of the water were swift-flowing. At the New York Public Library a few days earlier, in a book by Sanjeev Saith and Mukul Kesavan titled *A Journey Down the Ganga*, I had read these words about the river in Haridwar: '... as it hurries along, the river plays out its name, "Ganga", derived from the Sanskrit root *gama*—"to go". Thus the word Ganga means "swift-goer".' Back in my twenties, my mother had wanted to participate in the aarti performed in the evening, and she was elated at the sight of the diyas lit on small boats fashioned from petals and set afloat on the fast-flowing waters. But there was also some sadness that evening because after a fight with my parents two days earlier I had said that I wanted to leave home. This was after my college results had come out. I had done poorly. I hadn't really understood what I was saying; I had no idea where I would have gone. Maybe to the home of a friend whose father had given me a chance to file journalistic reports. My parents brought me to Haridwar for a night and then we had gone to see a holy man who lived on a high wooden platform and allowed his followers to touch his feet.

But here I was in Haridwar again; my parents were now both dead. It was morning and there were hundreds of bathers in the water. They held on to the steel railings and chains that lined the steps to the river. The sky was overcast. I stood on a bridge and watched the throng. Infants were getting their heads shaved and their mothers or grandmothers would walk down to the water to offer the hair to the river. Was it this sight that put the idea in my head to get my head shaved? I wanted to slip back into that mood again, and on my walk back to the hotel, I stepped into a small barbershop. Back in March, in Varanasi, following tradition, the barber had used no lather, only water from the Ganga, and his iron razor, to shave my head. Here in Haridwar, the barber, playing loud Punjabi music, spread a cape around my neck and front. It had a blond woman's face on it. Was it Taylor Swift? I didn't ask. The barber wouldn't have known. The geyser in the hotel bathroom wasn't working. But it didn't matter. With my head shaved, I now felt I had embarked on a spiritual journey.

Bathers, Rishikesh, 2023

The taxi arrived on time at nine. En route to Devprayag, we stopped first at Rishikesh. Large langurs—gray-haired monkeys with long tails—sat sedately on the riverbank. The river ran fast here. Cows and calves were everywhere. Also, of course, pilgrims. A young man with a wooden box that said EAR CLEANER approached me and offered to take a look at my ear but I shooed him off. I saw a group of young boys in the yellow garb of sanyasis being led by an older youth, similarly attired, but with thick glossy hair that looked extravagantly styled. This was a temple town and I soon had had enough.

The taxi-driver's name was Surender. At one point during the afternoon, he pulled up on the side of the road and asked me to step out. Trucks and a bus were coming up toward us but he said I should walk over to the other side. I did. Near my feet there was a deep drop down into a valley and I saw now what Surender had wanted me to see. There was a sort of a V below: from the left came a quick flowing green river and from the right there flowed down a muddier stream. This was Devprayag. I could see a single pilgrim several hundred metres below me bathing at the place where the two streams met. (An image from Tomas Tranströmer: 'two colors meet and flow into each other / on the wet paper of a schoolboy's painting.') The green waters were of the Alaknanda and the brown river was the Bhagirathi. Where they came together, the river became the Ganga.

Devprayag, 2023

I was probably being lazy when I reached for a metaphor—the two rivers coming together represented a mixing of difference to form a powerful newness. I was doing this not only because there were lotus flags of the Bharatiya Janata Party all over the state of Uttarakhand, or because there was evidence everywhere of the BJP's new offices in small towns—but because of the shameful political developments in the northern part of the state where Muslim traders had been asked by Hindutva warriors to close shop and move away. And what about the media? The unabashed servitude to majoritarianism is a part of this sorry tale, of course. If the Hindutva purists had their way, the Ganga would only be of a single colour, saffron. They wouldn't want the different communities to mix into each other; they would prefer that we make the other bleed.

After Devprayag, we had another hour's drive. I had thought that I had booked my hotel at Devprayag on an American travel site but I had made a mistake. So, we drove on and then came to Malakunti where, apparently, I had made the booking. We stopped on the side of the road and then had to cross a bridge on foot to check in. As there was no Wi-Fi, I put my watercolours and a notebook in a tote bag and went out for a walk in the mountains. The walk was exhilarating but also exhausting. On the way to Malakunti I had seen signs for white-water rafting, but there were no rafts on the river. It was explained to me by the hotel staff that this was because of the fresh rains. The river was swollen and too turbulent. The paintings I made didn't please me but the next day when I woke up in the minutes before dawn I sat down and made this painting.

Devprayag, 2023

Chamoli. We were driving toward Rudraprayag and hoped to reach Auli by the evening. Surender stopped at a cheap dhaba. There were no customers and there was also no power; we waved away flies that tried to sit on our faces and our hands. While I read a book called *Between Hope and Despair: A Hundred Ethical Reflections on Contemporary India,* Surender watched some sort of drama in Hindi on his cellphone. The drama had an insistent laugh track that I found annoying. After we had eaten, I took my wallet to the desk where the owner was sitting. Behind him on the floor, leaning against the wall, was a newly framed portrait of the prime minister, his smile fixed like a stare.

Soon, we were on the road again. The road winding through the mountains had signs put up by the Indian Army: THIS IS A HIGHWAY, NOT A RUNWAY. And also the more familiar signs warning of landslides and rockfall; sometimes, as if to illustrate their point, the signs had boulders and smaller debris scattered around them. Now and then Sikh men on motorbikes, triangular yellow flags flying from them, passed us on the road. They were on their way to Gurudwara Hemkund Sahib. On the side of the highway, statues of Lord Shiva appeared in several places—though not as frequently as the wreckage of cars and trucks.

By late afternoon we had reached Joshimath. Above this town, only half an hour away, was Auli, where our hotel was located. As there was an army post there, and their radar jammers made it very difficult to use the GPS, it wasn't easy to find the hotel. Each home, it seemed, had been turned into a homestay. After some difficulty, we found the place we were looking for. The hotel had a narrow garden overflowing with hydrangeas and tiny roses. On the other side of the thin road, the land fell away, sloping down into the valley. There lay the township of Joshimath spread out beneath us. And on the other side of the valley appearing impossibly close were the tallest mountains I had ever seen in my life. These were the mountains of what are called the Higher Himalayas: slabs of dark metamorphic rock rising higher and higher into the air, their tips and higher flanks covered with snow. Clouds moved slowly in the air below me.

I sat quietly on a chair placed outside my hotel room and sipped tea. The door of the room next to mine was open. A child was repeatedly screaming *Jai Shri Ram, Jai Shri Ram.* An older voice would now and then respond to the child by echoing the same cry. In another few minutes, the child, a boy of maybe five, burst out of the door. He carried a red plastic club and a red plastic trident. Around his neck hung a tiny amulet. When he saw me, he stopped for a moment, and came closer to look at the sketchbook I was holding in my hands. His moment of contemplation over, striking the ground near my feet with his club, he shouted again, *Jai Shri Ram, Jai Shri Ram.*

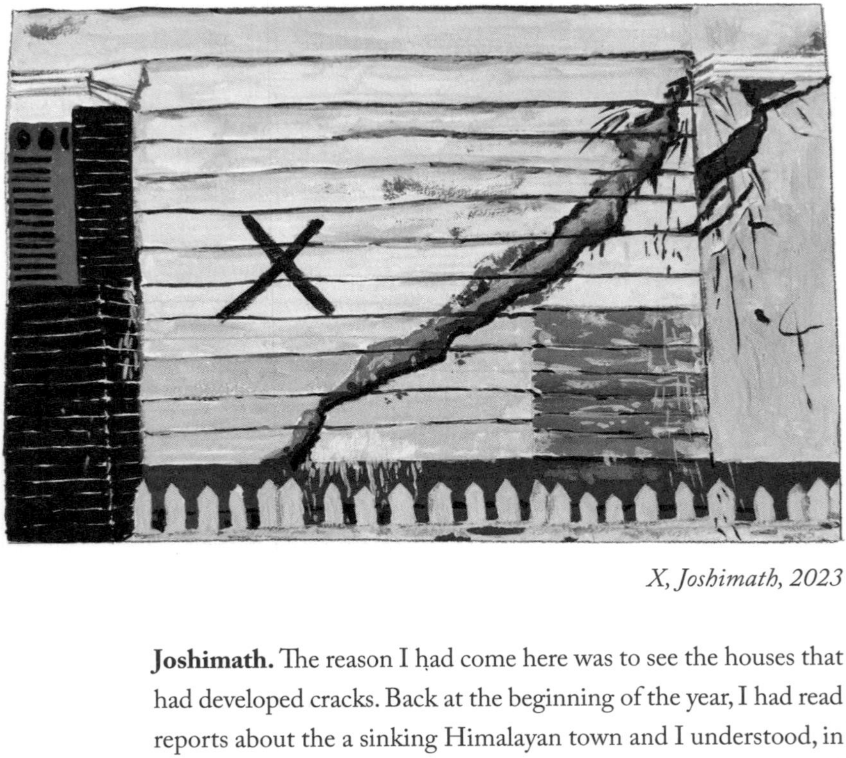

X, Joshimath, 2023

Joshimath. The reason I had come here was to see the houses that had developed cracks. Back at the beginning of the year, I had read reports about the a sinking Himalayan town and I understood, in a vague way, that the town's story was about skewed development and ecological disaster. Standing in front of the collapsed or tilting houses, the effect is plainer, more dramatic and devastating.

The damaged homes in Joshimath are identifiable not just by the cracks in their walls or even by the red X that the government has put on them but also, even from a distance, by their air of desolation and abandonment. This is the truth of Joshimath. Why did this happen?

Atul Sati, a local inhabitant and an environmental activist, told me that the first cracks appeared in a row of houses towards the end of 2021. By now, even by the government estimates, there are at least 868 homes affected. Sati took me to meet families whose homes had been destroyed. Ashish Joshiyal, a young man with his hair in a ponytail, said that a thin crack became visible outside his family home at the beginning of January this year. The next day, the crack had widened. So, the family moved out and is now living in a relief camp run by the army. Behind where Joshiyal stood, I could see how the family temple had snapped in two, the red dome fallen back while the rest of the structure had slid forward. His family owned an orchard—fruit trees were visible in front of the ruined structure, apple, orange, apricot, plum—but there too the ground had slipped. The earth was sliding down toward the Alaknanda, the headstream of the Ganga.

The plight of the people in Joshimath has everything to do with the river, or more accurately, with the blasting of the rock beneath Joshimath to build a hydroelectric project here, diverting the flowing waters of the Alaknanda into a tunnel to produce electricity. Sanjay Uniyal of the Joshimath Bachao Sangharsh Samiti explained to me what was involved in this process: for each blast, the power company drilled 157 holes in the stone foundation a kilometre below the earth's surface, the holes being 12 meters long and 15 to 20 centimetres wide. The holes were then packed with dynamite. Every 12 meters (or even less if the explosion was not effective), the process of drilling and dynamiting was repeated. As a result of the digging of the tunnel, the situation now is such that, as Uniyal put it, 'there is Joshimath beneath Joshimath'.

Later, I read a 2023 study published in *Current Science* about Joshimath and the surrounding areas. The report blamed rapid urbanization, obstruction of stream courses and lack of efficient domestic wastewater drainage system for the adverse impact on mountain ecology. The dangers that the researchers on the study were warning against were clear: 'The unscientific road alignment, construction of barrages and underground tunnels in the proximity of urban towns without any consideration of the geological fragility are amplifying the terrain instability.' What this means in less academic terms is that the ground sinking leads to cracks and collapsing buildings.

The reality of state capitalism is that it spreads devastation and calls it development. It was heartbreaking for me to enter the newly constructed home of Dinesh and Puja Rawat. The lower floor was still under construction. The upper floor was finished, beautifully furnished, and already the walls showed hairline cracks. Dinesh is a primary school teacher. He said that for people of his economic status there could be no chance of building a second home—he had poured everything into the building of this one. Every month when he took a substantial sum of money to the bank to pay his mortgage, he asked himself what he was doing, paying money for a house that he was sure will be demolished. When I was leaving his house, he showed me the door at the side of the house that is always left unlocked at night. That door was in the room where his boys sleep. If the house began to fall, that was the door to be used to escape. I tried to imagine living each day with the fear, and knowledge, of losing your home. I asked Dinesh if he and Puja talk of the problem and their strategies to deal with it. No, he said, if they talked about it, it made them feel helpless and full of despair. So they didn't, but they made it a point to join the protests and speak at the dharnas.

The Joshimath Bachao Sangharsh Samiti has been agitating on the issue of hydroelectric power plants on the river since its formation in 2004. In other words, the group has been protesting the state's misguided attempts for long before the current work near Joshimath. Sati is a veteran leader of the group and reminded me of previous disasters on the Rishi Ganga when not just once but twice floods on the river swept away the power plants under construction along with the labourers working on them. Sati described how unresponsive but also delusional the state continued to be on these matters; all the memos he presented to the local officials and sent to the chief minister about the sinking of the town went unanswered until the protesting citizens took out a torchlight procession and then blocked all traffic the next day on the national highway. The promised compensation from the government for all those who had lost their homes only came as a result of organized protest; what awaited resolution was the determination of other aspects of this disaster, for instance, where would people be relocated, what compensation would they receive for their lost land, etc.

Before I left Sati, I asked him to step out on the balcony of his house so that I could photograph him. Then, I asked him to write a statement, any statement. Please see below what he wrote. My bad translation of it is here: 'The mountain, earth, and the tree in front of which I stood to have this photograph taken, may such greenery live on in humans, in this mountain, and on this earth. To this end is, and may it stay, dedicated, this life ...'

जिस पहाड़, धरती और
पेड़ के आगे खड़े हो
यह तस्वीर खिंचाई है
यह हरापन, मनुष्य में
यह पहाड़, धरती बनी रहे
ऐसा ही इसी को समर्पित
है और रहे जीवन... अतुल सती

Auli. I woke up at dawn. The peak of Nanda Devi was covered by mist. Nanda Devi is the second highest mountain in India. The previous day the bellboy at the hotel had informed me that I'd be able to see the peak from my pillow. That didn't happen. But I was prepared to wait. Many cups of tea were drunk. And then, the clouds lifted and I was able to make a quick watercolour of the snow-covered peak. Then, I climbed into Surender's taxi for a five-hour drive down to Rudraprayag where I had booked a room. From Rudraprayag, we would drive down to Dehradun the next day because I had to catch a flight to Varanasi.

For this drive I had downloaded an audiobook of Geoff Dyer's novel, *Jeff in Venice, Death in Varanasi*. I remember that the taxi was leaving the outskirts of Joshimath when the actor reading out the novel narrated the following lines which made me grimace and chuckle at the same time: 'You grow older imperceptibly. Your knees begin to hurt perceptibly. They don't get better. Occasionally they get worse and then improve but they never get back to what they were before. You begin to accept that you have a bad knee. You adjust your walk to compensate and alleviate but, by doing so, you set the scene for lower-back pain.' We had only minutes earlier crossed Atul Sati's home. The previous day, climbing the high steps from the road to the house, my knees had hurt. To make things worse, the thin air had left me gasping for breath.

Overleaf:
Nanda Devi, Auli
2023

After a short while, Surender stopped to get the car's tires checked for air. And after we had gone a little distance further, we stopped again for tea. I was still listening to Dyer's novel and enjoying it immensely. The owner of the tea shop had his

6/29/23

hands buried in mud. He was moving his small palm trees from the ground into big pots. He washed his hands for a long time and then prepared tea for us. While pouring our tea, he casually informed Surender that the road was closed a few kilometres down. He said that the road had been washed away. Surender's face took on a pained expression. He said that he had been wondering for the past half hour why there had been no traffic from the other side.

I asked the men how long these stops usually lasted. It will take a few hours, Surender said. He guessed it would be evening by the time we reached Rudraprayag.

How much longer did we drive? Another half an hour or a bit more? Then, we reached the procession of stopped cars. During our drive that morning, we had come down from an altitude of 4,000 to 2,000 metres. It grew hot on the road and it was necessary to be in the shade. I went under a tree and continued to listen to *Jeff in Venice, Death in Varanasi*. Dyer's protagonist was at the Venice Biennale, complaining about the heat, but he was falling in love and, equally crucially, he seemed to have access to an unlimited supply of chilled Bellinis.

After another hour or two, Surender turned his taxi around and we went back to a town we had passed earlier. We could get lunch while we were waiting. Then we returned to the highway and the cavalcade of stalled vehicles. Miraculously, there was an opening in the line of cars. Surender had said to me that the line was now about eight kilometres long. By now, people had hung wet laundry out to dry. Others were sleeping under trees. The river flowed beside the highway and many of the stranded travellers had gone down to bathe or swim; they now looked like picknickers having a good time.

The afternoon turned to evening. I saw the stranded travellers playing cards, or watching videos on their phones, or taking leisurely walks holding cups of tea in their hands. I envied them a bit. There had been zero information from anyone remotely resembling a figure of authority, but it was known that a landslide ahead had caused the trouble. Machines were removing the rubble but more would slide down. I had been stuck there for eight hours when evening came. I had disappointed myself by not venturing out of the car to talk to anyone milling around. There was a preponderance of pilgrims in the crowd who had journeyed to places like Badrinath and Kedarnath. I told myself that I ought to have taken this opportunity to find out, for instance, how closely was Hindu religiosity aligned with a fondness for the ruling BJP? I wrote and uploaded a little Substack entry about this, confessing my guilt, thereby giving myself permission to not do anything more.

I was also feeling some anger. Literally in front of where our car was stuck, there was a tunnel being built in the foundations of the mountains. I wrote in my Substack entry that if I were in a mood to talk to anyone in the seemingly five thousand cars lined up there, what I'd have liked to know is whether they saw any connection between our plight and hydro-power projects like the one across the river from us.

One last point: when I had set out on this travel I wanted to

Hydro-power construction, near Chamoli, 2023

understand what was happening to the Ganga at different places. If I hadn't embarked on this journey, I wouldn't have been receiving this startling lesson: about landslides after rains and, as in a badly written story, have the experience of being stranded right opposite what I was seeing as the cause. This didn't alleviate the despair I was feeling; it only deepened it.

*

Chamoli and Varanasi. The highway where we had been waiting forever came alive at four in the morning. There were shouts and cheers. Cars were honking as if India had won the World Cup. We had been stuck for sixteen hours. I was awake and ready to leave. The previous night Surender had received a call from a man I had interviewed in Joshimath. This man had seen the news of the landslide on TV and suspected that I was stuck on the highway. Aware that I couldn't reach the hotel in Rudraprayag, he wanted me to get out of the car and walk a bit further on the highway to a small hotel named Tapovan. The hotel was owned by a friend of his, and he had arranged so that I could get a bed to sleep for a few hours. I did as he suggested. The room was hot but I could at least lie down. Only brown water came out of the tap in the bathroom and I was also forced to keep the windows shut because of the noise outside. For about three hours, I slept.

When the cars began to honk at 4 a.m., we joined the fray but were immediately caught in a jam. Impatient drivers were trying to overtake and to compound the problem, several of the vehicles on the road were without their drivers. Then, it began to rain. It was still dark. Surender said that the rain could cause another landslide. I had felt hopeful that I would be able to catch my flight that afternoon, and then I saw my hopes diminish as a half hour turned to an hour and we had barely covered a few hundred yards.

Yet, in fits and starts, we made progress. After more rain and more slow movement over a few kilometres, the road cleared. I heard the narrator of Dyer's novel say in my ear, 'There was something I was beginning to realize about India. There was always room. Even when there was no room, there was room.' We were again driving down the mountain switchbacks. Again, the familiar sight of Shiva statues and the wreckage of cars. By the time we reached Rishikesh the sun was shining bright and I saw more than a few rafts on the water. We had often passed other construction sites in the river valley. The familiar blue tin roofs and white walls of the offices, the long line of excavator trucks, the prefabricated concrete that were parts of the tunnel. Near Paoli, I saw a man step out of the mouth of one of the tunnels being bored into the mountain. He was miniscule—it was a sublime, terrifying sight. It was only at that moment that I realized how enormous the tunnels really were.

Ugly gashes in the mountain side marked other building sites. Why does construction look so much like destruction? Surender didn't want to risk stopping for lunch and we kept speeding toward Dehradun.

One cannot sign up only for the good things in life. Like the fine hotel room where I ended up at the end of the day in Varanasi. I told myself over and over that if I accepted this comfort, I couldn't say no to the discomfort I had experienced due to the landslide on the highway the previous day. It was, of course, easier to say all this when I was relaxed and happy. On the day that I had arrived in India, *The New Yorker* magazine had published a piece by the philosopher Agnes Callard titled 'The Case Against Travel'. One of the arguments that Callard's essay made was this one: 'Travel turns us into the worst version of ourselves while convincing us that we're at our best.' I had harboured no such delusion when I was stuck in the car for hours; in fact, I had observed my behaviour and found it lacking. But I also learned that villagers from the mountains above the highway had come down during the night with khichdi they had cooked for those trapped on the highway. Surender had also helped in a roadside hotel's kitchen, making tea. In other words, there had been a wider sense of the self, a feeling of community, and genuine good will. On the other hand, it was also true that the whole length of the highway where the cars had been parked for so many hours was littered with plastic, garbage, tiny red paper teacups, discarded foils and wrappers. The same goes for the drivers who prolonged our agony by racing forward, leaving no space for vehicles coming from the opposite site—I saw driving toward us, as if in a mirror, the same tired faces, the same air of uncertainty and fatigue dense like the mist from which the cars emerged.

Varanasi. I slept well, given how little sleep I had had the previous night, and then I showered. This latter fact deserves a paragraph of its own. Over the previous days, I had bathed out of a bucket in different bathrooms all across Uttarakhand. In each bathroom, the floor was littered with ant-wings and naphthalene balls. In one of them, the smell of urine emanated from the drain when the water went down, making me suspect that the drain for the shower and the septic tank were connected. But not in this bathroom, no, no. There was a pleasant smell of lemongrass and a range of so many options for soap! After my shower, I went to Pehelwan Lassi, and drank the sublime liquid from clay cups. What a fine, rich lassi is served at Pehelwan's. The broad, patient man standing next to the large containers will first ladle some yogurt into the cup and then place on the top a dollop of malai before sugaring it with rich rabri. All for sixty rupees.

Fortified by Pehelwan's lassi, I went to Lamhi. I was going to visit the ancestral home of the great Hindi writer Premchand (1880-1936). It was blazing hot. I was sitting in a three-wheeler, inhaling smoke and dust that was cutting my life short by several years—and the thought did pass through my mind that now that I had drunk Pehelwan's lassi, I could happily die.

At Lamhi, Premchand's home was found easily enough. A plain white building with semi-obscured government signboards. There was, as is appropriate for the home of a man who wrote social realist fiction, an air of dereliction about the place. A volunteer was at hand, a man finding a vocation after retirement. He has pasted edifying lines about the writer and his work on the whitewashed walls. The best touch of all, however, was that there were young men on the benches outside, either stretched out and asleep or nodding over books in their hand. I found out that they were visiting from surrounding villages and were going to take the test for entry to the police forces that afternoon. These youth had found the place because they were told that it was free like a temple but also very quiet. Did they know any of Premchand's stories? The question gave them pause but they had prepared for the General Knowledge section. Several of them recognized the name; only one of them could name any of his stories. I liked very much the simplicity of these young men, their need, and their desperation.

As often happens to famous people, it was Premchand's fate to be remembered in his birthplace also through several painted portraits. One of them was, as far as I could gather, an attempt to portray a young Munshi Premchand. The drawing below is my pale imitation of the portrait I saw there. It was stuck to a warped cardboard under a thin transparent plastic cover; moisture had seeped in at the edges, particularly the right-hand corner, but even that could not distract me from the fact that the famous writer in this painting appeared to lack a mouth. Gogol might have been made famous through his association with the nose; our own Premchand in this image seemed resigned to be associated not with the power of the pen but with the sheer scale of his moustache. I have been overwhelmingly negative. I need to acknowledge that while the artist, probably an amateur like me, might have committed grave atrocities against a few of Premchand's facial features, he had also endowed him with a halo to show respect.

Never mind that the halo now resembled a puffy moon, or maybe a marshmallow dissolving in an inky marsh. Pasted to the portrait were two slips of paper, both bearing the same instruction, Do Not Touch.

Kalam ka sipahi, Munshi Premchand, 2023

Next I went to Manikarnika Ghat. I almost turned back; actually, I turned back more than once. Back in March, I had come there with my sisters and other relatives with my father's body. We had cremated my father in the early afternoon. I entered the narrow lane leading to the ghat at around the same time as we had done in March. I was trying to see whether I remembered everything. I had forgotten some details but everything came back to me now with vivid force. The narrow lanes, the two-wheelers with their loud horns, the tiny shops selling items needed for worship, or tea and sweets, paan shops, even a mobile phone repair shop. I recognized the psychedelic paintings on the walls, the cow dung splattered on the ground, the low wires. It all looked familiar and I saw myself slipping into sadness.

We had carried my father's body on its bamboo bier through these lanes on his last journey. On this current trip, I decided, without thinking about it, to become a journalist with a notebook. What can I say about my visit to Manikarnika? I didn't cry there. I hadn't cried in March either, not at the ghat; there was just the grim resolve to get done with the rituals. I played the journalist now, asking questions about the price of wood. One maund is around forty kilos. The cost of one maund of wood comes to five hundred or six hundred rupees. A lighter body requires five maunds of wood, a heavier body or a body that has been in a hospital, and has been filled with water and other liquids, like my father's was, requires seven to nine maunds of wood. The terrible, guilty reality of our use of wood when the electric crematorium is available. I had read somewhere that 1,200 square kilometres of forests are cut down each year in India just to burn bodies. What are the problems that you are facing, I asked the dom who provided the fire on the khar grass for the funeral pyre. Mata Prasad Chaudhuri was a dour, middle-aged man, who noted down on a ledger the names and amounts of money received from the mourners to whom he gave the burning piece of wood. Chaudhuri replied that the politicians hadn't kept their promises, more space was needed for funerals. These were questions that I didn't need to ask and already had answers for. I was seeking distance even though the real reason I had come back was to feel close to my father. *Where have you gone, where have you gone …* Such words would form in my head. It was intensely hot. I craved coolness and water. Mourners, all men, stood around me in small groups or sat on the steps in the shade. They were waiting for the cremation to be over, for their loved ones to become ash and air. I remained observant and made more notes in my black journal but back in the hotel room, next to the fine-smelling bathroom, when I texted my sisters to report on my visit, the tears came. Now, once again, I was a grieving son and brother.

In the evening, I took in the awful spectacle of the evening aarti on the river (everything is a spectacle in India these days; mostly because of its politics) and then had the most pleasant conversation with Vishwambhar Mishra, the mahant of the Sankat Mochan Mandir, about fighting pollution in the Ganga. I had long ago read about his celebrated father's fight to save the Ganga: the story of a man who was a civil engineer as well as high priest. The current mahant is cast in the same mould as his father; he is a professor of engineering during the day and a priest by night. He was critical of all that the government had not done and was as unsparing of what it has managed to do. I had recently been a witness to what the political and business elite had wrought in the Himalayan reaches with its plans to divert the Ganga. Here, the mahant told me, there had been similar disasters. Not just with the question of pollution but the administration's experiments to assist business and money-making. The government had dug a canal here in the sandy bar on the opposite bank of the Ganga so that they could send bigger cruise boats up the river. It didn't work. They tried to build something they were calling Tent City. The river swept that away too. These attempts to make changes that are merely cosmetic were always going to fail. Moreover, they appealed only to people who were looking at the Ganga from far-off places like Delhi. The point was to save the Ganga for those who actually bathe in it and want to touch its water with their lips.

The mahant had printed out a chart of the readings taken on the local river water a week earlier. The level of faecal coliform bacteria found at the ghat where the river entered Varanasi was 29,000,000/100 ml and where the river left the city it was 62,000,000/100 ml. The acceptable level for water fit for drinking is 50/100 ml. (If a gloss were needed, here is Geoff Dyer: 'Everything in Varanasi was taken to a delirious extreme.') The mahant drew a different lesson from the horrifying readings of the water quality. Unlike the government, he didn't want to say that the whole of Ganga was polluted. Instead, the truth is that the river was most polluted where raw sewage was being emptied into the water. That was the lesson of the difference in the readings between the ghat where the river entered the city and the ghat where it exited Varanasi. The sewage entering the river ought to be treated before entering the water and it ought to be diverted to a point in the river downstream from the city. Every river has self-cleaning properties, the mahant told me. If the river is given a chance to breathe again, it will live again.

Mahant Vishwambhar Mishra, Varanasi, 2023

Not even a drop of sewage should be allowed to reach into the river channel. Ganga ji is clean always. We should not pollute.

01.07.2023.

Darbhanga Ghat, Varanasi, 2023

Varanasi and Allahabad. In the morning I was still in my hotel in Varanasi, coming out on the balcony to paint a scene inspired by what I could see outside, and then in the afternoon, I took another Vande Bharat train that brought me to Allahabad. Sitting in the train, I read and made notes. At the station I was met by Udbhav Agarwal, the author of *A for Prayagraj*, a biography of the town I was now visiting; it had recently been renamed Prayagraj. A few years ago, Udbhav had been my student at Vassar College and he wrote parts of the book in a class of mine. Udbhav and his father first took me out on a boat to the site of the sangam, where the green waters of the Yamuna join the muddy waters of the Ganga. (Udbhav's family priest was accompanying us on our boat ride. He said that the waters of the Yamuna were 'blue' and that the waters of the Ganga were 'milky' and I could see the poetic truth in what he was saying.) Udbhav's book ends with his grandfather's death; the old man is in the ICU in a Delhi hospital when he says he wants to go back home where the rivers meet. The doctor tells him he won't survive the journey but he insists he will. After landing at the airport, he is taken to the sangam, after which he comes home and bows before the photographs of his parents and the family deities before he lies down on his bed and dies.

*

Allahabad. The day started with a hunt for kachauri and jalebis. Udbhav's father was ready when I woke up and Udbhav joined us soon. We went to the town's old alleys in our search for good food. Paalu Namkeen Bhandar. Loknath Jalebi Bhandar. Sulaki Lal Shrinath and Sons on the Old Grand Trunk Road. We ate everything. Khasta kachauris, jalebis of different kinds, puris and aloo dum, halwa ...

In the afternoon I went to meet a government doctor. There had been numerous reports during the second wave of Covid, in the summer of 2021, about corpses floating in the Ganga. The BBC had reported that the river was 'swollen with bodies'. The doctor I was meeting had overseen medical care for the past three decades during the gigantic Kumbh Mela, one of the largest gatherings of humanity on the planet. What was his experience during the pandemic? In May 2021, it all started with seventy-one corpses washing up on the riverbank at Chausa near the Uttar Pradesh–Bihar border. After that, there were more bodies. And also bodies found in shallow graves on the banks of the Ganga near Ghazipur. Dogs and crows were feeding on the exposed corpses. I recited all these facts but the doctor didn't see any point in talking about these things. He said that the death rate was very high during that phase of the pandemic; relatives often left the bodies on the banks of the river and then the administration would take care of the cremation. As a member and former head of the Allahabad Medical Association, he wanted to tell me that the doctors had worked around the clock, even volunteering at a building which had been turned into a hospital. It seemed to me that I was being given the official, sanitized version. I turned the conversation to the Kumbh Mela. How is the river kept clean during the gathering when tens of millions assemble on any single day? He said that sanitation was the biggest challenge. There was a twenty-four-hour monitoring of the water quality, especially for fecal E. coli, the setting up of sewage treatment plants, efficient collection and disposal of garbage.

Earlier in the day I had asked Udbhav to take me to see an old friend of mine and his wife. My friend's name was Ramji Rai; I had met him in Patna in the nineties when he was editing the Hindi magazine *Samkaleen Janmat*. He was a leftist activist, a 'whole timer'. His wife, Meena Rai, had recently retired from her job as a teacher. I had read on social media that she was now giving all her time to managing the production of *Samkaleen Janmat*. We walked through a narrow alley and then entered a small apartment. Soon, the air conditioner was switched on in their bedroom and that is where we sat and talked. Wasn't it amazing, I later asked Udbhav, that we had come through a dirty alley, smelling of rot and filth that lay strewn about us, and entering this room we found a man who spoke so easily and fluently to us of everyone from Firaq Gorakhpuri to Virginia Woolf to Slavoj Žižek? Ramji Rai had been an indefatigable cultural and political activist; I had long admired his sensitive, literary sensibility as much as his ideological commitments. But I had also known for a long time that none of that work would have been possible without the work and support of his wife. Meena Rai had been a teacher for forty years and I asked her to tell me about her struggles. She told me the story of a fight for her rights—as a daughter-in-law, as a wife, as a teacher. When I was leaving, I took a picture of the couple and asked Meena Rai to write a few lines about her life. Here is my translation of her statement: 'I like putting my ideas into practice even in my private life. If one is doing work that is appealing, then you don't feel tired. After I became a managing editor at *Samkaleen Janmat*, my blood pressure returned to normal and my headaches vanished. I also made my own space in society with *Samkaleen Janmat*.'

(Meena Rai died in November 2023 after a brain haemorrhage.)

अपने विचारों को अपने निजी जिन्दगी में भी लागू करना मुझे पसन्द है। अपने मन का काम करने में थकान नहीं होती। समकालीन जनमत का प्रबन्ध संपादक का जिम्मा लेते ही मेरी बी.पी. व सिर दर्द की बीमारी अपने आप खतम हो गई। मैंने समाज में अपनी पहचान भी 'समकालीन जनमत' से ही बनाई।

मीना राय

Meena Rai, Allahabad, 2023

Patna. The Rajdhani Express brought me to Patna shortly before dawn. It was not yet five in the morning but my elder sister was awake and waiting for me when I reached our family home. She was a doctor and led a busy life; I felt guilty and told her she should go back to sleep. I don't know whether she did but I was able to fall asleep very soon. This was the same bed where I had slept when my father was in the hospital for two weeks in March. This used to be his room and if I opened the closet I was sure his clothes would still be hanging there. After sleeping for two hours, I went to the park opposite our house. Another repetition here, this was my father's morning routine. My sisters had kept vigil at the hospital and every morning I had bought yellow rashbhari berries for them from a woman among a line of vendors outside the park. The same woman was there but now she was selling purple jamun. I hadn't eaten jamun for years. I paid her fifty rupees for a small bag. After my sister left for the hospital, I began to get ready for my trip to the Ganga. In the hallway, I saw that my sister, as was her habit, had lit a lamp under my mother's photograph. But now there was also my father's photograph there. You come back home—in place of a person, a photograph.

The weather app on my phone said that it was 93 degrees Fahrenheit (33 degrees Celsius) but 'feels like 122 degrees'. Somewhat confusingly it added that there was fog outside, but that was wrong. It was a haze in the air that lay on you like a warm blanket that you couldn't kick away. I walked beside the Ganga on the promenade and then took a boat to the other bank where parwal and karela were being cultivated. Tea in clay kulhars was being sold from a hut; while having my tea,

I examined the pile of plastic bottles and other trash on the banks which would soon be drawn into the river. In his book *A Goddess in the Stones*, Norman Lewis writes: 'At Patna, the Ganges, fed by important tributaries, becomes very wide, a placid unruffled flood, green and opaque in the shallows, then lightening to the milky aquarelle of the distant shore, with its line of palms, on this occasion, sketched in on a ribbon of mist.' But that was a description of the river in winter. Now, swollen by rain and silt, the river appeared vast and brimming to the full; there was nothing much to be seen except the brown waters and a few floating bits of water hyacinth.

At places like Krishna Ghat, there was a general sense of indolence among the people sitting or sleeping under the stone umbrellas, but those bathing in the river seemed full of good cheer. On the promenade were spread to dry green, faded scrubs and mauve-coloured T-shirts embossed with a medical logo and the words Popular Health. Just a few minutes earlier, I had passed masses of people around the Patna Medical College and Hospital—small, thin women with infants in their arms, old couples looking lost, two men supporting an older man in the middle, a youth helping free a rat caught in a metal fence—and now it was nice to witness people seeking pleasure. After the tea, I thought I should return home. Patna was shimmering in the haze. Why had I even come here? I remembered taking the ferry with my parents and my sisters as a child to cross the river on our way to our ancestral homestead. In interviews I have spoken about my desire at that time to be able to draw the boats I saw on the river. I wasn't able to do it. Years ago, I had also cremated my mother's body on these banks. Then, just a few months ago, I had stood on the banks with my father; I was angry with him, I thought he had been rude to a journalist who had come to talk to me. I didn't want to now think of such memories. I waited on the boat, sitting in the baking sun, for our return to the ghat. To do something, I sketched the boat moored a little distance away. Soon the boatman was collecting money from all of us; he was also trying to convince a younger man to buy his boat for two lakh rupees. It was hot and not even noon but as the vessel chugged to the other side the boatman took furtive sips from a small dark bottle. After each sip, his voice rose higher. In another hour, after a visit to a bank, I was home. My sister hadn't come back from the hospital yet. I sat down in the hallway under the photographs of my parents.

Ganga paar, Patna, 2023

When he died, we took my father's body to Varanasi. He had once told my elder sister, after watching some show on TV, that he wanted to be cremated at Manikarnika. After the cremation, I had waded into the Ganga with his ashes. I was fulfilling my father's wish. There was no greater meaning to the act. A little later I was asked to bathe in the river to mark the completion of the rituals. The water was dirty; I had just cast bones and ash into the river. One of the priests allowed that I could walk a bit more downstream. The water was indeed a bit clearer there. A man was already bathing a little distance from the slippery steps. I asked him if the water was clean and he said yes before proceeding to spit in it. I felt I couldn't turn back. And I went in too. I cannot say that I wholly shared the feeling described by Atul Gawande in *Being Mortal* when he took his father's ashes for immersion in the Ganga—and yet how could I possibly be wholly distant from its basic sentiment? Here is Gawande: 'Although I didn't feel my dad was anywhere in that cup and a half of gray, powdery ash, I felt that we'd connected him to something far bigger than ourselves, in this place where people had been performing these rituals for so long.'

*

In the morning, fairly early, I left Patna by plane. There wasn't time to have breakfast; I ate a mango from a tree that grew in our front yard. When had my father planted it? It had been a very short visit to Patna. One night only. I could not pretend that my bond with my hometown remained unchanged; something had ended with the death of my parents. Had there been more in Patna, I wouldn't have gone to other places on the Ganga. The previous night, however, my elder sister had summoned a paralegal to the house. A thin man in a shirt and jeans had come over a little before dinner. He explained what we would need to do to claim our inheritance: the division of the house which my father had built and the remaining land that was in his name in our village. It all seemed very complicated to me and I didn't know how much strength I possessed to battle Indian bureaucracy.

Less than three months before my father died, I had brought my son to spend a few days with him. It was wonderful to see the two of them together. A few days after my return I published a poem, in the original Hindi as well as in English translation, in a magazine. The poem was accompanied by a photograph of my son hugging my laughing father—and a note with the following words: 'I belong to a generation and, perhaps more important, a social milieu in which we didn't talk to our fathers. We were more intimate with mothers; our relations with our fathers were formal. We also don't talk much about death. We have a superstition that it would court bad luck. But our greater reticence, I feel, is about love. It is not that love is hidden—the stoic father who gives money to the son going away to college, and asks if he has eaten or if he has kept the railway ticket safely, is showing love—but it is seldom expressed in language. I became a writer to point out what was left unsaid, not so much to unsay it as much as to gesture toward it. I wrote this poem after my recent visit to my father in Patna. I was accompanied by my thirteen-year-old son, Rahul.' My poem was titled 'Conversation'. Here it is:

In two years my father
will be ten short of turning hundred.
It is not easy to say:
You should get your will prepared
otherwise
there will be problems
for everyone later on.

But it is more difficult to say
those things
that my own kids very easily say
in the other language:
'Dad, I love you.'
'Dad, I miss you.'
'Dad, don't go.'

Poetry makes nothing happen: my father didn't leave a will. But it was reported to me that he had seen my published poem. He had become emotional and told my relatives that he would get the will done that very evening. Perhaps a part of him didn't believe that he was going to leave that quickly. In fact, after his death, my nephew found a recent entry in my father's diary. He had given himself eighty-eight years and seven months. Which meant that when he died, falling ill suddenly, he had imagined he still had six more months.

When the plane took off from Patna, I looked at the Ganga outside my window. And when the plane got ready for its descent in Kolkata, I saw the river again, now called the Hooghly. I had first gone to Kolkata, then still known as Calcutta, to get my visa from the American consulate. Later, as a graduate student at an American university, I had returned to watch Badal Sircar's street plays and to conduct interviews with writers like Mahasweta Devi. Whenever I arrived in the city, an outsider with his roots in the provinces, I was reminded of scenes from Satyajit Ray's *Aparajito*, the second film in the Apu trilogy. Apu arrives in the city as a young man from the village; he is a student and takes up a job in a printing press to survive. He is immersed in his new life and neglects his mother who waits for him in the village. I had left Patna and gone abroad to study. That was more than three decades ago. Every year I came back to see my parents, and they never complained about my choices, but the guilt of abandoning them never left me. I'm in a crowd somewhere, at a conference or a party, and then I suddenly remember that my mother is waiting. I leave the gathering and rush toward the train. But the train is already leaving. How often had I woken up in my sleep from a nightmare of this sort? Too many times to count.

On this visit, unlike Apu in *Aparajito*, I didn't get to lounge beside the river. I didn't lie on its banks, smoking, talking to a friend. I took it in from afar. After arriving in the city, I saw the river from the Vidyasagar Setu. About twenty ferries lay on the river's surface in a torpid haze. On the other side of the bridge, looking in the direction of Rabindra Setu (what used to be called Howrah Bridge), there were another twenty ferries lying seemingly immobile on the brown water. Long ago, before the river's silt made travel by big vessels impossible, the East India Company ships had sailed up this part of the river and established their trade settlement here. (It is difficult for me to make an imaginative link with the past; I need more historical learning. The day before, standing beside the Ganga at Krishna Ghat in Patna, I learned that the site had served as a battleground on 3 May 1764 between the British and the combined forces of Shuja-ud-Daulah, Mir Qasim and Shah Alam II. I couldn't go back to that distant past; my mind stopped at the memory of those names that I had encountered maybe in my ninth or tenth standard History class. Oh, the fatal boredom of one particular teacher's voice, his maddening lilt, my fellow students ...)

My second encounter with the river was when I drove out to Bandel to look at the Hooghly Imambara. There the river was in fierce flow. In the distance loomed the Jubilee Bridge. A young man standing at the water's edge warned me not to go too close. I asked why. He said, 'Jwaar bhata.' The tide from the sea! The salty water of the Bay of Bengal reaches the river here. One day, and how soon, will it also cover this land?

*

Bali Island, Sundarbans Delta. The car that picked me up at seven in Kolkata passed a huge garbage dump and then several small towns—a couple of busy wholesale fish markets, and what appeared to be a wholesale jackfruit market. Also a cattle bazaar with several Muslim cowherds who in states like Uttar Pradesh and Haryana would have been lynched for taking calves away on carts. In a town called Gadkhali, there was a boat waiting for me. In his book *A River Called Titash*, the Bengali writer Adwaita Mallabarman describes, in Kalpana Bardhan's translation, the rural countryside of his birth in the following words: 'The bosom of Bengal is draped with rivers and their tributaries like tangled locks, streaked with the white of foamy waves.' But I hadn't passed any rivers, only the wetlands near Chowbhaga, and a polluted canal with makeshift lavatories built over them, the lavatories nothing more than burlap wrapped around a bamboo platform. On both sides of the wide highway there were palm trees, banana, bamboo, neem, gulmohur, bougainvillea and mango trees. Fields had been turned to fishponds, with green or blue fishing nets spread over them. I later learned that many of these ponds contained brackish water piped in from the sea. This allowed for the farming of tiger prawns and large crab.

In Gadkhali, I was led to a boat. The mainland was behind us. The boat's name was 'Jungle Prince'. I was offered water and asked to sit on the small sofa. Soon, as the boat drew away on the Bidyadhari river, the same breeze that was making the water ripple on the river was also riffling my hair. I felt every part of my body relaxing. I was aware that as sea levels keep rising, the islands in the Sundarbans will be drowned. There are over a hundred islands in the Sundarbans, more than half of them are inhabited by people. There are five million people in the Sundarbans on the Indian side of the border; on the other side, in Bangladesh, eight million. In a few years, scientists believe, climate change will be responsible for the largest human migration in history.

An hour's journey by boat would bring me to the camp where I was to spend the night. But first I was to be fed. In the boat's hold, there was a cook! He made me luchis and aloo dum, also an omelette. I was given tea with wild honey from the Sundarbans, and bananas, and sandesh. As it was high tide, the small trees on either side were partially under water. Occasionally a boat would pass in the opposite direction, mostly carrying huge bottles of drinking water. Large boats designed for tourism lay anchored here and there—I had arrived during the low season, hardly no one visits during the monsoon. It began raining after a bit and then stopped. I took pictures and made notes.

The camp was on Bali Island, one-storey buildings overlooking ponds fringed with palm trees and hibiscus bushes. One of the ponds had provided the three-kilo fish which was served for lunch. Other items included a saag made from banana flower. The mango pickle was from fruit harvested from the tree growing outside the eating enclosure. I understood that I was being served an experience that was curated as local and ecological. This also meant that the camp had no air-conditioning, and my skin felt sticky with sweat. For a while there was no electricity, and then there was the sound of a generator kicking to life. When the fan started moving, I fell into deep sleep. It was four in the afternoon by the time I woke up. Outside my window, the wind was slowly shaking the leaves of a banana tree so that they resembled the ears of elephants.

I went for a tour of the village on a three-wheeler. The panchayat elections were in two days and the flags of the Trinamool Congress fluttered everywhere. The three-wheeler passed a large concrete building; it was the cyclone shelter. Back at the camp, a sixty-five-year-old local farmer named Anath Misri was waiting. He talked about the many cyclones he had experienced during his lifetime (1980, 1986, 2009, 2018, 2020). He said that the river had changed over the past ten or fifteen years; erosion had changed the character of the river and widened the basin. Silting and subsidence had cut off the smaller rivers from the Ganga that used to feed them fresh water. There was less sweet water available; the water had turned saline. Migration from these cyclone-affected islands with rising surrounding sea levels was alarmingly high. Anath babu said that ever since a nylon fence was put across the stretch of the opposite island where the mangrove forest provided a home to the Royal Bengal tigers, there were fewer tigers swimming across to this island. He had had three encounters with the tiger but had escaped unscathed. The government mandated that when fishermen went into the mangrove forests there had to be at least three of them in the boat. Anath babu believed that what was required on the part of each of the three persons was full alertness and coordination. Any slip could be fatal.

I went to sleep reading about tigers. In one article, according to official statistics, over fifty fishermen were carried away by tigers each year. This meant an average of one attack each week, but it was also true that not all killings are reported. Any entry into parts of the terrain dubbed 'core areas' by the government was considered illegal and the victim of a tiger attack was not eligible for compensation. This made any attack in those areas less likely to be reported; you wouldn't want to put yourself on the wrong side of the law.

A 2016 article in the *Indian Journal of Psychiatry* reported that in the Sundarbans there were three thousand 'tiger widows', women whose husbands had been killed by tigers, and they suffered from discrimination and cultural stigma.

Sundarbans, 2023

For hours I sat on the small sofa on 'Jungle Prince'. The view I had was of the prow of the boat advancing into the waters of the rivers and the water channels that make up the Sundarbans. I had woken up shortly before six. A compact man in a camouflage shirt was already waiting for me. He was my guide, a naturalist armed with a pair of binoculars and a book in a blue plastic cover, a book about the birds of the subcontinent. Mostly what I would see today were birds with names shouted out by my guide. Lesser Whistling Duck, Red-whiskered Bulbul, Ashy Woodswallow, Blue-tailed Bee-eater, Streak-throated Woodpecker, White-breasted Kingfisher. You get the picture. But going down the Gomdi river and then meeting the river Bidya, I felt as free as the river terns flying in the air. Once again that fine breeze and the sun not yet raising a heat-mist. In the distance, where five small rivers met, a row of tiny fishing boats standing still. Everything was okay with the world, and the day was full of possibilities.

The guide kept using the word 'sighting', which is an abstract word but was being used to designate something very specific and concrete: the appearance in one's field of vision of a creature, either swimming in the water or stalking the land, more precisely, a large creature with a reddish-yellow fur and black stripes with a quick and lethal ability to kill. The possibility of a 'sighting' was still there, and I recognized it, of course, as part allure, part dread. All the energy on the boat seemed focused to this end and I began to feel a bit distant from it; I questioned myself even as I felt this emotion, I wondered whether it was a fatalistic resignation on my part, whether I had decided that if this goal was so fervently desired, I'd rather not be a part of it. We saw a monitor lizard, several spotted deer, varieties of crab. And yes, the names of all the birds were being recited and I was often handed a pair of binoculars but it was getting wearying to be thinking that everyone was thinking *This is not it, this is not it.*

The low tide had exposed the tangled roots of the mangrove forest, not just the roots but also the spiky pneumatophores that help the trees breathe when water covers their trunks. The slopes were silty and shiny with wetness; fiddler crabs and other forms of life crawled over the mudbanks. I was served breakfast: parathas, pickle, egg, mango; the food made me drowsy. For much of my adult life, a nap has served as salvation, a retreat from all my woes. I voiced these thoughts aloud and was informed that there was a bed below the deck. This turned out to be entirely true. I went down and slept. No need of a noise machine because the boat's engine was making a helpful, consistent racket. With this welcome sleep I had avoided the tiger. I assumed that the tigers of Sundarbans (I was told there are about 115 of them roaming the forests presently) were also avoiding me. I hoped they, too, were napping in the shade.

When I woke up, the tide was coming in, the green water from the sea mixing with the muddy waters of the river. Just the previous night, in my warm room with the fan whirling above me, I had read in Arati K. Rao's book *Marginlands* the following description of the Sundarbans, which were 'teeming with Bengal tigers; saltwater crocodiles; venomous, constricting snakes; endangered birds; primates, crustaceans, monitor lizards, river sharks, river dolphins, anadromous fish, wild boars and deer, all superbly adapted to a life on the brink of brine.' I had occasion to think of all that amazing variety of creatures but also, of course, of the people who lived among them. I had only seen a few of the humans, in the distance. This was when we had started our journey in the morning. The guide had pointed at them with his binoculars. There were women in the water, close to the shore, trolling for 'tiger prawn seeds'. It was a dangerous job, the guide said, because there was always the threat of crocodiles and river sharks. And, of course, the tiger.

In due course I was also provided lunch. The Bengalis have this maddening and also endearing way of serving food in courses. You are given rice with dal and one kind of vegetable. Maybe also salad. You start eating and think that it would have been nice to have one more dish. Well, there is more! You are next given a kind of spinach and then another vegetable, all of it locally sourced. You are now feeling heavy. But then the main course arrives, this delicious fish soaked in a delectable gravy. You are ready to get up from your meal by now but you can't. This is so good, you say to yourself, wondering why this fine fish wasn't served first. Finally, the meal is over and you are about to stagger away drunkenly like one of the flies that has been trying to land on your plate. But no, there is more! The cook smiles and says chutney, chutney and he ladles this sweet mango thing on your plate. It is great. When you get up, there are anguished cries from the cook. Fresh curd, fresh curd.

Sundarbans, 2023

I went down below the deck again. This time I tried to sleep, couldn't, and read for a while. The pilot of the boat kept placidly steering it through the interconnected waterways. This whole expensive exercise was for my sake, and I felt I was being wasteful. But I didn't have the energy to do anything, much less protest. When I came up much later, the boat was motoring through the waters. The tide was full and the sun was hot on the deck. Wild mynahs were landing on the boat's railing, their beaks open as if for water. The guide was poised alertly, his binoculars scanning the horizon.

*

Kolkata. My journey along the river was coming to an end. The previous night I had returned to the city. Earlier I had intended to go to Gangasagar, a delta town on the edge of the sea where the Ganga empties into the Bay of Bengal. But then I was advised to not travel on this day because of village panchayat elections in Bengal. Later I would learn that nineteen people had died in clashes among rival groups across the state. The violence had included not just the looting of ballot boxes or 'booth capturing', but also bombings and shooting. One ghastly report was about a party worker dragged out of his house and his neck cut beside a pond. Nevertheless, I felt my journey had remained incomplete. Not only had I avoided danger, but I had courted comfort. I had checked into the Tollygunge Club.

I had read about the club in Jhumpa Lahiri's novel *The Lowland*. In Lahiri's story, starting in the 1950s, we follow two boys, brothers, who want to explore the Tollygunge Club.

They first head 'toward the paddy fields, where the Adi Ganga once flowed, where the British had once sailed boats to the delta.' We learn that the river was now stagnant, silted, and lined with settlements of refugees from East Pakistan. Then, the boys arrive at the club. They use kerosene tins to cross over the high boundary wall. 'Suddenly, they were no longer in Tollygunge.' The trespassers are surrounded by massive trees: cannonball and eucalyptus, bottlebrush and frangipani. There is grass that is 'uniform as a carpet, unfurled over sloping contours of the earth'. The boys had been told that though Nehru was the prime minister, a portrait of Queen Elizabeth still presided in the main drawing room. This was the place where I was rooming.

After breakfast and a couple of hours spent in the club's library looking at books about the city, mostly enjoying the photographs taken of the filmmaker Satyajit Ray on his sets, I went down to meet Sugata Hazra whom I had invited for a chat. Chairs and tables were set on gravel: we sat under umbrellas with giant fans blowing. Hazra, a genial man, short and bearded, was a retired professor of oceanographic studies and an expert on the Ganga Delta. He wanted to sit outside so that he could smoke while drinking his cappuccino.

Hazra had been studying oceans and rivers for decades and said that in 2015 there was flooding before extreme drought and in 2023 the same pattern was being repeated. Conditions in 2024 would be worse, he said. Earlier, there used to be one or two major cyclones in ten years; now there were two such cyclones in a year. But, Hazra said, we continue fighting and keep entering into endless negotiations, and schoolkids will be directed by NGOs to make posters, and folks like me will write articles from which people will learn how serious things are and they will still go in droves to shopping malls. What is one to do then? For writers and artists like me, Professor Hazra had some advice. Instead of making sci-fi films like *Avatar,* we should write novels that refine our perception of nature, he said. Why do you feel happy when you sit beside this green grass, he asked, pointing to the lawns next to us. He wanted me to emphasize the link to something larger, and also the symbiotic relationship that binds us to the world around us, a world where not everything has been either monetized or weaponized.

Back in 1996, Hazra had been conducting research in Antarctica. He described a scene to me: during nights where the sun never disappeared, he would be alone surrounded by kilometres of unending snow, and he would shout loudly the words of Rabindranath Tagore's song, 'Mahabishwe mahakaashe mahakalo-maajhe / Aami maanabo ekaki bhromi bismaye, bhromi bismaye.' (Here's a translation from the original Bengali that Hazra said I could find online: In this wide world, under this immense sky, / Amidst his all-encompassing time, / I, a mere mortal, roam all by myself and wonder!)

Before he began to study the oceans and rivers, Hazra had worked as a geologist. He said that as a geologist he knew that humans have been around for a very short time. We were a very young species and we were destroying ourselves and others. There were many, many other species on this planet and even when we were gone they would probably go on living and they would regenerate the planet. But if humans were to live, we had to stay in harmony with nature. I thought this bit of gyaan or wisdom was worth repeating as many times as we can.

I had read somewhere that Charlotte, Viscountess Canning, wife of the first Viceroy of India and, like me, an amateur watercolourist, had written: 'I now feel I have seen India.' I could not make that same earnest and presumptuous claim, of course. I had wanted to take a trip through some of the towns and cities on the Ganga, and, as I said before, I also wanted to feel closer to the memory of my father who had died some months ago. There was always the impulse, or the temptation, to say something conclusive or momentous about places or people. I couldn't arrive at any singular feeling, however. Tagore's sense of wonder was certainly also mine but I was never far away from the anxiety brought about by climate change. Or a simpler, more direct rage at the delusions of development. Also doubt. In my non-fiction classes I teach a piece by Ryszard Kapuściński called 'Snow in Ghana'. It is an account of his stay overnight at a village in Ghana after his car's tires have blown out. The head of the village, the nana, wants to know what is snow. He wants to know more about Poland. Kapuściński makes an attempt to be accurate but is haunted by the inadequacies of his account in that unknown Ghanaian village. (Having said what I have said, what have I really said? There is so much more!) This is one of the paragraphs in the essay 'Snow in Ghana' that I emphasize in my discussions with students and point to its more open, more ambiguous ending: 'What I had described was not my country. Now, snow and lack of colonies—that's accurate at least. But it is nothing, nothing of what we know, of what we carry around within ourselves without even wondering about: nothing of our pride and despair, of our life, nothing of what we breathe, of our death.'

In fact, the lesson of reading Kapuściński is to be alert to the necessity of actively pursuing knowledge. The legendary travel writer's first trip abroad was to India. This was in 1956. Recalling this trip many decades later, Kapuściński was to write that his visit to India had afforded his 'first encounter with otherness'. His stay in India had also been 'a great lesson in humility'. He wrote: 'I returned from that journey embarrassed by my own ignorance.' What was one to do in such a setting? At least for the outsider, and who wasn't in some small way always an outsider, the right thing to do, according to Kapuściński, 'is to prepare oneself thoroughly for such an encounter'. India wasn't as alien to me as it was to Kapuściński; I was born in India and grew up to adulthood there. But I had been living abroad for decades; each year, when I undertook a journalistic task to write about India, it had become for me a means to connect with my past. It was not enough. For some years now, a desire I have had as a writer was to slip into the dream-life of ordinary Indians and—as if I were stepping into a wide and mighty river—immerse myself in its flow and come back gasping for air.

Many Words for Heat, Many Words for Hate

Two summers ago, during a trip to Delhi, I asked myself if Virginia Woolf, whose travel notebooks I had been reading in London, ever wrote about the heat while she was travelling in Italy, Greece and Turkey. I asked myself the question but I could not remember. I could remember nothing in the terrible Delhi heat. There were days when the temperature was over 8 degrees Celsius higher than normal. The previous month had been the hottest since India started keeping records 120 years ago. People dying from heatstroke; schools closing early or simply shutting down; power outages. As I said I had been in London, at the British Library, looking at Woolf's notebooks from her travels over 1906–09. When I bought my own notebook at Heathrow, I made a little calendar in plain imitation of how Woolf had drawn her plan of travels during October 1906. Milan, Sienna, Perugia.

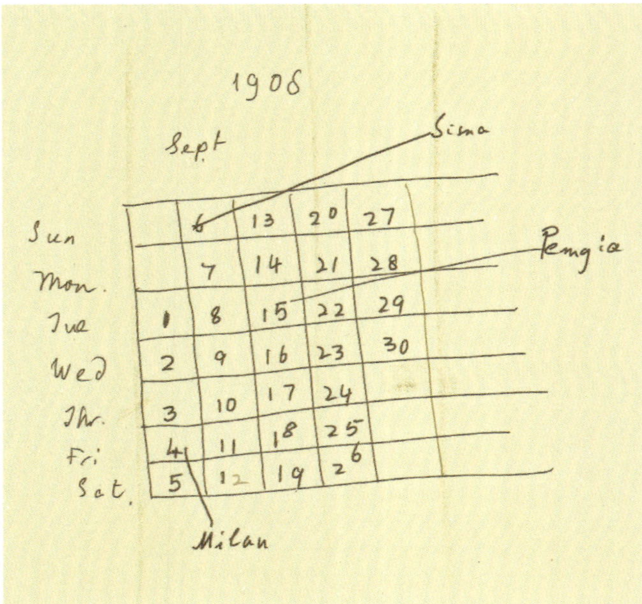

In Delhi, the heat was chemical, something unworldly, a dry bandage or heating pad wrapped around the body. I sent a note to my friend Ravish, who was at that time still an anchor on NDTV's Hindi show *Prime Time*. I asked Ravish that if the Inuit supposedly have more than fifty words for snow (a *specific* word, for example, for snow used to make water), why don't we Indians have more words for heat? Ravish asked members of his audience to respond to this question. Words and phrases that Ravish and I didn't know, in a mix of Indian languages, came in from different cities and parts of the country, adding nuance and variety to what the newspapers were only calling a 'heat wave'. Ravish concluded his monologue by saying that if you forget the many words for heat in your own language, you will also forget the names of your neighbours or the fact that people of two different religions used to live peaceably together. You will also forget why you are beginning to forget.

*

My publisher provided a car for me to go to bookshops and sign copies of my books. At one point I passed a billboard that showed a fighter jet in the sky and above it these words: *Join IAF and give your career a flying start.* That Indian Air Force ad hadn't changed for forty years. I remembered seeing it from the DTC bus windows in my late teens, and how, because I lacked any sense of direction, I would imagine myself in a jet, my head in the clouds.

There were new billboards too. A ubiquitous one was that of Arvind Kejriwal, Delhi's chief minister, sitting in a yoga pose on green grass. The ad promised that a yoga teacher would be in touch if you called the number provided. Nehruvian secularism, with its separation of state and religion, was now a thing of the past; more dangerously, religious identity, specifically a Hindu identity, was being conflated with the national identity. On the campaign trail, Kejriwal recited from Hindu prayers and sponsored government-paid pilgrimages for the elderly from Delhi, most egregiously to places like Ayodhya, where a sixth-century mosque was demolished by a Hindu mob in 1992. No one, not even an opposition politician like Kejriwal, who could stand outside the Hindutva fold, dared show a distance from what was fast becoming—no, what had already become—the culture of dominant majoritarianism. Hindutva, in its hard-edged form, is unsparing. As an ideology of ethnic absolutism, it decreed that India was only for Hindus. (During the riots in Delhi in 2020, one of the slogans was *Hinduon ka Hindustan*—India is for Hindus.) In this scenario, yoga was only soft Hindutva.

A journalist friend told me that in his youth he watched Hindi films in which the hero, invariably an angry young man, wreaked havoc on his enemies. When the film ended, my friend would step out of the cinema hall feeling superhuman, his nerves tingling. He was telling me this story because, he said, *that* was the feeling now gripping the BJP's followers. They imagined themselves as the protagonists in a powerful story about the destruction of their enemies. There was a Ram Navami procession in Delhi that my friend had watched, a traditional occasion celebrating the birth of Lord Rama, who has been adopted as the reigning deity of the BJP's campaign for a Hindu nation. The crowd in the procession was chanting anti-Muslim slogans. My friend looked up from where he stood and saw two young women filming the procession on their mobile phones from a high balcony. It would be normal, my friend said, for these upper-middle-class women to feel uncomfortable when confronted with open displays of thuggish behaviour. But not the two he saw on the balcony. Their faces shone with enthusiasm. Each one pumped a fist in the air. The women reminded my friend of what he was like as a teenager, his imagination fired by a delusional masculinist fantasy projected on a screen.

*

Umar Khalid is a young scholar and activist who earned his doctorate from Delhi's Jawaharlal Nehru University. Khalid has been jailed since September 2020 under the UAPA (Unlawful Activities Prevention Act), which allows the government to detain individuals without trial. A number of arrests made under UAPA in recent years have been of the government's critics, journalists and activists. Khalid is accused of inciting riots in Delhi in February 2020, in which fifty-three people died, many reportedly at the hands of Hindu mobs.

I wrote a letter to Khalid, which a friend forwarded to his lawyer. I had heard that Khalid had read more than a hundred books in prison. *Umar, can you tell me what you have been reading?*

*

My wife's name is Mona Ali. She is a Pakistani national. Her uncle, who died in Delhi recently, was a retired police officer. For decades, this uncle—whom she called Chacha—had kept a daily diary. This was of interest to me as a writer and a diarist. I remembered that I was present at Delhi airport, back in 2001, when this gentle, old man met my wife, his younger brother's daughter, for the first time—they had always been separated by a border. Two decades ago, my wife was allowed a visa to visit India, and so she travelled from Pakistan to Delhi. At the airport, Mona and Chacha hugged and cried while I stood and watched on the side.

During the summer visit two years ago, I asked Chacha to read to me his diary entries from December 2001. He had accurately recorded my wife's arrival on the seventh, but the prose was emotionless. No mention of heartache, or the tears that I'd observed. I too made an appearance. Chacha's entry for the thirteenth of December read: 'Terrorists attacked the Parliament. Waiting for Mona and her husband to visit us.'

Chacha's eldest sister had left for Pakistan the year after the Partition. He didn't see this sister again till he retired from the police and was able to travel to Pakistan. In other words, Chacha wasn't able to see his Qamar aapa between 1948 and 1992. How was their first meeting after that long separation? What did he write in his diary? While I was making my unsuccessful search among the stacks of his diaries for the one from 1992, Chacha told me that those who had lost their siblings during the riots that accompanied the Partition were, perhaps, luckier than him. Their loss was final; his loss had lingered, tearing him apart as one year stretched into another, decade after decade.

I then looked at Chacha's diary from the year 1979. At that time he was a senior officer, a deputy inspector-general of police, in eastern India, in Shillong. He was helping build a police academy there. On the nineteenth of January he received a telegram from his brother in Pakistan, informing him that their father had died a few days earlier. Chacha's father lived in India, but he occasionally visited Karachi. (Such travel was possible at that time.) The news of his father's death left Chacha bereft, and he wanted to call his mother. When he booked a trunk call to Karachi at the local post office, he was asked what language he would be speaking in. He said it would be Urdu. A few minutes later, the operator called to say that no interpreter could be found. Each phone call to Pakistan had to be monitored, and no Urdu speaker was present in Shillong. As a result, Chacha wasn't able to talk to his mother. Speaking in English now, he told me that the irony was that at that time he was in charge of the entire border that India shared with Bangladesh and what was then still called Burma.

Chacha recorded in his diary the receipt of the telegram from his brother on the nineteenth. I went back to the page for the thirteenth of January. On the top he had written 'Holiday. Second Saturday.' And then, 'Listened to cricket commentary all day.' Underneath, in a clearly retrospective entry, he had drawn a rectangle and noted within that space the following words: 'Abba passed away today.' Often, I make the mistake of thinking that diaries reveal secrets; the truth is that as often they reveal silences. There was no mention in Chacha's diary of his failed attempt to offer condolences to his mother.

Chacha's diaries, 2022

The week before I had arrived in Delhi, there were accounts in the news, and especially on social media, of bulldozers being used to demolish Muslim homes in Delhi and elsewhere. The visiting British prime minister, Boris Johnson, appeared on my timeline because he had jumped aboard a new JCB bulldozer in a factory in Gujarat. The JCB bulldozers were the ones being used in the demolitions. Did he not know that people's homes were being destroyed?

In more recent news, a feminist activist had tweeted about a Hindu man being publicly killed in Hyderabad for marrying a Muslim woman. The Hindutva brigade was using this incident to further spread anti-Muslim hate. The activist responded, pointing out that the *bhakts* had done the same thing, celebrating the killing of a Muslim man, Dilshad, who had married a Hindu woman.

I mentioned the above tweets at a small gathering of my extended family in Patna. We were sitting around drinking lemon tea. Someone said that a nephew of mine had been having an affair with a Muslim girl from Kashmir. The boy's mother interrupted to say that she had been relieved when they broke up. She had been scared that he'd be killed by the girl's family. Then I was asked if I remembered an incident from my boyhood. We were in our ancestral village at that time because it was winter break. Did I remember a distant relative of ours, a young woman, who had died because her infected appendix had burst inside her? I didn't remember. It didn't matter. The truth was now being revealed to me. There had been no burst appendix. The girl had been killed by her own family. She had made the mistake of getting involved with a Muslim classmate. The relative who was telling me this story learned this years later when she was at medical school. A fellow student told her that his best friend had been that girl's lover. He didn't know how the girl had been murdered, but he had seen what they did to the boy's body. Try as they might, they couldn't find enough pieces to make a decent corpse.

*

Patna. I was invited to speak at a college that I used to pass every day on my way to school as a boy. At that time, I understood that this particular institution was a breeding ground for goons, but my father had informed me that the college was now among the best rated in Bihar. When asked to choose a topic, I said I would talk about keeping a diary. I wanted the students to write down what they saw around them, and to record what was happening to them. (Was I thinking about the students? Not so much. I was thinking about who I was when I used to live close to the college. I wrote nothing then. My days were never connected in a story I could use to narrate what was happening in my world.) The organizers had been good enough to follow my request and give everyone in the audience a sheet of paper. There were three prompts from my side:

1. 'Yesterday it rained and today ...'
2. 'During the pandemic ...'
3. 'I want to tell the writer ...'

I should perhaps pause and first tell you that unlike any lecture or reading I have done before, there was a complicated ritual I had to follow at this college. The organizers asked me to remove my shoes and then place rose petals before the portrait of the politician after whom the college had been named. Next, flowers were presented to me, and a beautiful silk shawl draped around my shoulders as a gift. When this had been done, and duly applauded, I was given a lit candle and asked to light a lamp. While I was doing this, the men and one woman who were on stage with me placed their fingers lightly on my arms, so that we were all symbolically linked as we lit one wick after another. It was like a Hindu prayer ceremony, and it was remarkable to me that this wasn't seen in any way as being out of the ordinary at a secular educational institution. Lengthy introductions followed. It was only later revealed to me that the founder of the college, the principal, all the heads of various departments at the college, and indeed, also the day's honoured speaker, belonged to the same upper caste. We hadn't yet made the great leap forward into modernity.

When I arrived back at my father's house, I was curious to see what the students had written. In response to the first prompt, many had noted the renewed heat of the day. To the second, many wrote about the suffering and deprivation experienced during the pandemic, particularly by Bihari migrant workers. The responses to the third prompt were puzzling. Most students left that part blank. The first two prompts had asked for concrete responses, and they were easily provided; the third prompt was open-ended and required a more abstract and maybe even an imaginative response. It was difficult not to conclude that the students for the most part had nothing to say to the visiting writer.

But a few did. I had read to them a passage about a human rights lawyer who, speaking in Delhi to those protesting against unjust citizenship laws targeting minorities, advised everyone to keep a particular kind of diary: 'Keep a record. Don't trust the state. Don't expect the police to document the violence it is raining on your head. You have to do this yourself. Note it down.' Several students at this college wanted me to know ('I want to tell the writer . . .') that the protesters in Delhi were engaged in an illegal activity. In other words, while most students had nothing to tell the writer, those who did only wanted him to know that to protest against the government was not only anti-national, as the BJP leadership claimed, but also unlawful.

*

Delhi. I returned to the city to participate in two book events before catching my flight out to New York. During the day I had several meetings with journalists, editors and publishers. One reputable editor, who asked me not to name him, told me during lunch that his role was a narrow one. In a country 'where writers are semi-skilled, where reviewers are semi-skilled, where readers are semi-skilled', his task was to bring in technique where there was no technique. He had a near-nationalistic pride in Indian publishing which, he believed, is no longer beholden to the Western market. At the same time, he was critical of the ruling dispensation. Every year that the present leadership remained in power, India was regressing ten years, he said. The nation's pluralist ethos was in tatters. Writers ought to share the blame for this. There was a time when writers had clout—he used the French word *éclat*—but now they merely inhabited an echo chamber of irrelevance. He didn't blame the poor either. 'If you are a lower-caste rickshaw driver,' he asked, 'why would you vote for anyone other than Modi? To them, he is one of us.' The editor pointed at my plate and drink. 'Your tribe is eating linguine and drinking New Zealand white.'

*

Another friend bought me dinner after my book event at the India International Centre in Delhi. Then he showed me the handwritten reply that Umar Khalid had sent to my letter, in which I had asked him about the books he had been reading in prison. In tight handwriting, Khalid had neatly provided a list of nearly thirty titles. He had divided the list into two: fiction and non-fiction. Franz Kafka's *The Trial* and George Orwell's *1984* were among those on the first list; Ngugi wa Thiongo's prison memoir and Trevor Noah's account of having been born a mixed-race child in apartheid South Africa were on the latter.

*

Hours before my flight to London, I visited Arundhati Roy at her flat. The heat was nearly unbearable. In the early evening, the road was lit up with the yellow flowers of the amaltas, which made me think of Arundhati's unforgettable descriptions in *The Ministry of Utmost Happiness* of the brilliant yellow flowers defiantly saying fuck you to the hot brown sky. Arundhati had just prepared cold nimbu-paani, and I drank a glass quickly. The question I put to Arundhati was a simple one: What is common life in India like in the time of Modi?

A few days earlier, Arundhati had spoken at an event where G.N. Saibaba's book of poems—a kind of prison diary—had been released. The author himself wasn't present. This was because Saibaba, a professor of literature and a human rights activist, lost both his job and his freedom after being detained under UAPA, the same law under which Umar Khalid has been kept in prison. In the case of Saibaba, the conditions of incarceration were particularly horrific. He was kept in solitary confinement despite being ninety per cent physically disabled. On the day I met Arundhati, Saibaba had decided to go on a hunger strike because the authorities were not even allowing him to keep a plastic bottle for water, despite the incredible heat. (After his release in March 2024 this year, Saibaba told the press, 'It is a wonder that I came out of jail alive.')

Arundhati recounted to me, as a way of answering my question, what she had told the audience at the Saibaba book event. In the 1960s, she said, revolutionary movements in India talked about the redistribution of land and wealth. In the nineties, things had been reduced to campaigns against the displacement of the poor in places like the Narmada valley during the construction of big dams. From redistribution to 'let us please hold on to what little we have'. In the 2000s, it came down to the National Rural Employment Guarantee Act, which assured the poor one hundred days of unskilled manual work every year. Even that was considered by some to be unviable or unnecessary. Today, people were being forced to either fight for their very citizenship, or to rejoice at being given five kilos of flour and one bag of salt with the prime minister's picture printed on the front. India was like a plane flying backwards, with all its parts falling off.

Were the prison doors going to open for jailed human rights activists like Umar Khalid? Arundhati replied that it was difficult to know if it was more likely for them to come out and join the people outside, or for those waiting for them outside to join them within the prison walls. 'I don't want to scare you,' she said, 'but all these people in prison have sat at this table. Whether it is Gautam Navlakha, Sudha Bharadwaj, Varavara Rao, Rona Wilson . . . It is so chilling when you speak at press conferences in Delhi, because all the people who used to speak on such occasions are not there anymore. What we are seeing more and more is prisons being filled with journalists, lawyers, academics, intellectuals, activists, students.'

Arundhati had one last point to make before I left. She wanted me to know that India wasn't controlled by an individual, it was controlled by the party to which that individual belonged. 'This is not Modi's India. This is RSS's India,' she said. The Rashtriya Swayamsevak Sangh is the right-wing party that held on to a dream of an undivided India ruled by Hindus. Modi had begun his political career as a grassroots preacher for the RSS. According to Arundhati, the RSS has approximately 15 million members along with women's organizations, schools in which millions of children study, farmers' and workers' unions. It has penetrated every single institution in India. She told me, 'The RSS is a nation within a nation waiting to take its place on the world stage, possibly in 2025, which will mark its hundredth year.'

*

2025. On my flight home I thought of this date often—for it is also the year the World Meteorological Organization predicts that the world will break a crucial heat barrier, making it nearly impossible to achieve what the Paris Climate Agreement had set as a goal, to limit global warming to 1.5 degrees Celsius by 2100. It's a dire prediction, and one that is not difficult to imagine coming true. If the slide into hate is just as irreversible in India, life, for a lot of people, is likely to become hell.

Central Park in May, 2024

The Green Album

'All is leaf.'
— Goethe

Canadian Goldenrod, Vassar Farm, 2022

After sunset, Poughkeepsie, 2022

Caleb and Timi, Poughkeepsie, 2022

Same-sex wedding next door on the day Roe vs Wade was overturned, 2022

The Nature of War

Where is the friend's house?

Poughkeepsie, 2024

'There it is! I recognize the window and the broken tree outside! Now let's find the friend.'

Poughkeepsie, 2024

Is there anything more ruinous for our planet than war?

In early January 2024, there was a report in *The Guardian* about the carbon emissions from Israel's war in Gaza, stating that a study had revealed that the 'first months of conflict had produced more planet-warming gases than twenty climate-vulnerable nations do in a year.'

Ninety-nine per cent of the 281,000 metric tons of carbon dioxide released during the first sixty days of the war could be attributed to Israel's aerial bombardment and ground invasion. The study did not include other planet-warming gases such as methane. Another significant detail was that almost half the carbon dioxide emissions were due to US cargo planes flying military supplies to Israel.

The report also carried this somber note: 'Previous studies suggest the true carbon footprint could be five to eight times higher—if emissions from the entire war supply chain were included.' Advancing this point of view, there was also a quote from Benjamin Neimark, a co-author of the study, who had said: 'This study is only a snapshot of the larger military boot print of war … a partial picture of the massive carbon emissions and wider toxic pollutants that will remain long after the fighting is over.'

Many more months had passed since I read the report, and the bombs had continued to fall. On homes, on hospitals, on refugee camps. Back in 2009, John Berger had written: 'Gaza, the largest prison in the world, is being turned into an abattoir.'

Now, as the months had passed, after the more than forty thousand dead, we could see that Gaza was turned into an abattoir once again and then razed. From this distance, it appeared to have been turned into dust.

From the newspapers I learned a new word: 'domicide'. Domicide (*noun*): The mass destruction of dwellings to make a territory uninhabitable. Those who managed to evade death, these hapless survivors had been forced into a crowded corner in Rafah where air-dropped food sometimes led to more deaths. And then in May came the news of the bombing of Rafah.

We could go on talking, with justifiable reason, of the carbon emissions from this devastating war, but can we talk of the *children*?

I heard a pediatric intensive care doctor say on the news: 'There's an acronym unique to the Gaza Strip: WCNSF. Wounded Child, No Surviving Family.'

On 11 January 2024 I read: 'More than 10,000 children have been killed by Israeli airstrikes and ground operations in Gaza in nearly 100 days of violence, according to the Ministry of Health in Gaza, with thousands more missing, presumed buried under the rubble.'

On 1 February 2024 Mohammed Hamouda, a father of three, told CNN that people in northern Gaza Strip were 'suffering a lot'. And added: 'They eat grass and drink polluted water.'

On 28 February 2024 I read that a two-year-old named Khaled Hijazi died in Kamal Idwan Hospital in northern Gaza because his stomach could not handle animal feed. Israel had cut off food and water supply for the entire population.

On 14 March 2024 I read that 14,861 children in Gaza had been killed by day 160 of this insane, intolerable war.

On 21 March 2024 there was a report published in *The New Yorker* about 815 medical evacuees from Gaza to a house in Doha. A line from the report that crept into my social media feed over and over again was the following one: 'This is the biggest cohort of pediatric amputees in history.'

A detail I will always remember from that report is that the medical staff put the severed limbs of the children in cardboard boxes, labelled the box with masking tape on which they wrote the name of the child and the body part, and buried them. Sometimes, the wounded children were too young to know their own names.

Except that in a story like this there are always other details to remember.

A fourteen-year-old lost his leg after being trapped under the rubble: he had spent a day under the debris holding the hand of his dead mother.

Gazal, aged four, who also lost her leg, was playing with a Barbie dressed as a bride. She folded the doll's plastic left leg behind her and marched her around on her right. 'This is

Gazal when she gets married,' she announced.

On 26 March 2024, on the front pages of *The New York Times* there was a picture of a small child, her right leg amputated, surrounded by medical staff in green scrubs. In the column alongside on the right was a report about a United Nations Security Council resolution calling for a ceasefire. That report included quotes from the Israeli top officials signalling their intent to continue the war.

In the inside pages was a report about sixteen young Palestinians—all but one younger than fifteen—being the lucky ones airlifted to Italy for medical treatment. 'The evacuees make up only a tiny fraction of the thousands of civilians, including many children, who have suffered grievous injuries ...'

Among them was a five-year-old amputee named Shaymaa Shady. She had survived an explosion. Again, a detail to remember: 'Shaymaa was rushed to Nasser Hospital, where doctors decided to amputate. They no longer had anesthesia, alcohol or other means to clean the wound, forcing the doctors to rinse it with murky water.'

Tens of thousands of such stories that remain untold. Tens of thousands of such stories that have died.

Why measure carbon emissions—why even try to save this world—if we cannot save the children?

Olive branch 1, 2024

Olive branch 2, 2024

Kites for the poet Refaat Alareer, 2024

Killed in the Gaza war by Israel's bombs, Alareer wrote in a farewell poem:

'if I die you must live / to tell my story'.

The same poem urged readers to make a white kite so that a child awaiting 'his dad who left in a blaze' should see the kite and believe, for a moment, that 'an angel is there / bringing back love'.

Rules of Writing

Sea, Montauk, 2023

I wrote a poem in Hindi first and then translated it to English. In Hindi, the title I chose with the help of my friend Satyanand Nirupam was *'Sach Chucchha Hota Hai'*; the title in English was 'Rules of Writing'. Why did I write the poem in Hindi first? I can't answer that question with any certainty. I did it perhaps because I was very clear in my mind that I was speaking to an audience in India and I didn't think what I needed to say was limited to English-language readers. It was gratifying for me when the poems were published on the Literary Activism website where the editor, the writer Amit Chaudhuri, provided the following note as a preface: 'Kumar is a novelist, photographer, artist, and, on the evidence of the Hindi poems he has been writing in the last two years, a bilingual poet. The poem below (which the author has also translated into English) is a one-off: a balanced consideration of countervailing positions that segues, unexpectedly, into manifesto. It raises a question that's suppressed in Indian Anglophone writing: the importance of mausam, or the "weather" (and everything that the word implies), to those who are mahaj lekhak or "mere writers". Mausam seems to mean an aspect of the everyday. If we are to subscribe to the poem's account of the Gandhian temperament, it would appear that most Indian liberals today are mahatmas: "great souls" preoccupied with "searching for the truth" who are unmindful of "the ringing of a bicycle's bell". Invoking the curmudgeonly, problematic Naipaul, the poem presents a much-needed argument against the idea of the "great" shortly after it pays Gandhi its respects.'

Overleaf:
Sea, Montauk, 2023

सच छूछा होता है

महात्मा गांधी की आत्मकथा में
मौसम का कहीं ज़िक्र नहीं,
लंदन की किसी इमारत या
सड़क के बारे में कोई बयान नहीं,
किसी कमरे की, कभी एकत्रित भीड़ या यातायात के किसी साधन की कहीं
कोई चर्चा नहीं—
यह वी.एस. नायपॉल की आलोचना है।

लेकिन मौसम तो गांधीजी के अंदर था!

तूफ़ान से जूझती एक अडिग आत्मा—
नैतिकता की पतली पगडण्डी पर ठोकर खाता,
संभलता, रास्ता बनाता बढ़ता हुआ इन्सान!

अगर आप सच की खोज कर रहे हैं,
क्या फ़र्क़ पड़ता है कि
सूरज आज शाम 6:15 पे डूबा कि 6:25 पे?

लेकिन नायपॉल की बात सर-आँखों पर!

अगर आप महात्मा नहीं
महज लेखक हैं,
आपको ध्यान देना होगा
नोट करना होगा,
अपने आसपास की दीवारों पर
खरोंचे गए प्रेमियों के नाम
छतों पर गिरती बारिश की बूंदों का अंतराल
आँधी में झूमते पेड़ों की डालों का लचीलापन
साइकिल की घंटी की आवाज़

या फिर दंगे के बाद का सन्नाटा
लिखना होगा,
कैंटीन में चुपचाप बैठी युवती के बारे में
जिसके सामने रखे पानी के गिलास में
पूरी दुनिया उलटी दिखाई देती है।

Hudson River, Metro North, 2024

Rules of Writing

Nowhere in Mahatma Gandhi's memoir
does he mention the weather
or describe London's streets
its houses, or even a room, the crowds,
no discussion of any mode of transport—
this criticism has been made by V.S. Naipaul.

But the weather was inside Gandhi!

A solitary spirit caught in the storm
a lone self
walking, stumbling
making his own moral way!

If you are searching for the truth
how does it matter
whether the sun set this evening
at 6:15 or at 6:25?

But I do heed V.S. Naipaul!

If you are not a Mahatma
and merely a writer
you will have to pay attention
and take note of the lovers
whose names are scratched
on the walls that rise around you
the interval between the drops of rain
being blown on the roof

the lithe branches of trees dancing in the wind
the ringing of a bicycle's bell
the silence after a riot.

You will have to write
about the young woman sitting alone
in the canteen and the glass of water
in front of her in which the whole world
appears upside down.

Hudson River, Metro North, 2024

Writing a Novel with Pictures

I was sitting in a train, travelling from my home in Poughkeepsie to New York City, when the idea for my new novel, *My Beloved Life*, had been conjured in my mind. During that journey—I'm talking now of something that happened nine or ten years ago—I was reading Denis Johnson's marvelous novella *Train Dreams*. It tells the story of an American railroad worker at the start of the last century. *Train Dreams* is a slim book but it has the feel of an epic. Maybe that fact had also inspired me.

I asked myself, what would the story be like if this ordinary man had been born not in Idaho but in India? My father was a small boy when India became independent from British rule. He had been born in a hut in a village in Bihar. His life had gone through many changes, and it struck me that in telling the story of a single, seemingly unremarkable life, one could possibly be narrating the story of nation or an entire century. The idea formed in my mind even before I had left the train that I would one day write about my father.

1.

A novel is by its nature fiction, but what happens when you put a photograph in it? A photograph is seen as having a documentary status, and it could be argued that it introduces the sense of the real, or of the non-fictional, in a novel's pages. Near the beginning of my novel *Immigrant, Montana*, a young immigrant from India in the 1980s hears Dr Ruth on the radio. My narrator was new not only to America but to that foreign land called adult sexuality. The first photographs in the novel were the twin portraits of the sexpert Dr Ruth and her Indian counterpart Dr Mahinder Watsa.

My caption for the photographs returned the reader to what is the work of fiction, a certain play, creating a world of make-believe. My protagonist's declaration that Dr Ruth and Dr Watsa were, in a sense, his real parents, was a work of imaginative refashioning.

Not my parents, but my forebears nonetheless. Dr. Ruth and Dr. Watsa, who ushered me into a world lit with the light of new knowledge.

A man with red marks on his body

2.

By the time my next novel, *A Time Outside This Time*, came out, I had been making watercolours. I had been moved by a photograph I had seen in an Indian newspaper—moved enough to want to paint it. The newspaper photograph showed a man kneeling in the dirt, begging for his life. Half of his vest and his face were soaked in blood. He was surrounded by onlookers—we see their legs, not their faces. The man on the ground, who has not been lynched yet but would be soon, was Mohammed Naeem. He was suspected of being a kidnapper. He was asserting his innocence, because that was the truth, but it was already too late for the truth.

In making a painting from the photograph in the newspaper, I was trying to look at the scene more closely. And perhaps make others do the same.

The above words belong to my narrator but, of course, they are also mine. That novel was about the spread of misinformation. In trying to understand the role of fiction in the age of fake news, I didn't think novelists needed to go back to facts. Instead, we had to alter our relationship to what is taken as the truth. Introduce ambiguity where there is a terrible, authoritarian certitude. My narrator asks a question: 'Why must one slow-jam the news?' and his answer is: 'Because all that is new will become normal with astonishing speed.' It is my opinion that W.G. Sebald's use of old, smudgy photographs and postcards that had been Xeroxed and made less legible was aimed at this ambiguity. He was destroying the link between visuality and truth even as he was reaching for and employing the visual artefact in his work.

3.

In recent times, when I visited my hometown and went for a walk near the house where I had grown up, I could see from the startled expressions of people that they had mistaken me for someone else. No, not someone else—they had mistaken me for my father. My hair had turned greyer than my father's and, for a moment or two, such was the degree of resemblance between us, it was easy to confuse one for the other. I had a sharp sense that I had grown old and that my father would soon die. Maybe this was only a fear but it had settled as a preoccupation. Then I happened to see a painting by the well-known Indian artist Atul Dodiya, a portrait of the artist's father. And my first thought was: *When I write a book about my father, this will be the cover!*

In Dodiya's striking painting, simply titled 'This Is Father', the painter's gaze is direct and the subject returns the look with equal directness. I say that the painter's gaze is direct because his look is unsparing, he paints his shirtless father in a naked light, as it were. He captures his age, his gauntness, his paunch. Even the choice of his palette—a near-depiction in black and white—seems designed to promote a way of seeing that is starkly real. The father's look is equally direct, he meets the painter's eye in a straightforward way. The father doesn't smile; he isn't here to charm or seduce. What you see is what you get. We could say that his look is accepting, neither aggressive nor evasive. The painting shows us a man who is looking with a calm objectivity not at us but at death itself.

A remarkable feature of the painting is the tube that extends out from the father's abdomen. When Dodiya made this painting, his father was in his early eighties and suffering from an enlargement of the spleen. His belly would get bloated and Dodiya would take his father to the hospital to get the fluid sucked out. When I first saw this painting, my father was also already in his eighties. I was very conscious of his mortality. Recently, Dodiya told me that his father was a civil contractor. He used to say that to construct something is difficult and takes time—while to destroy takes no time at all. The most tragic event of his life, Dodiya's father believed, was the assassination of Mahatma Gandhi. In 1999, Dodiya started work on a series of paintings about Gandhi called 'An Artist of Non-Violence'. His painting of his father was executed in 2002.

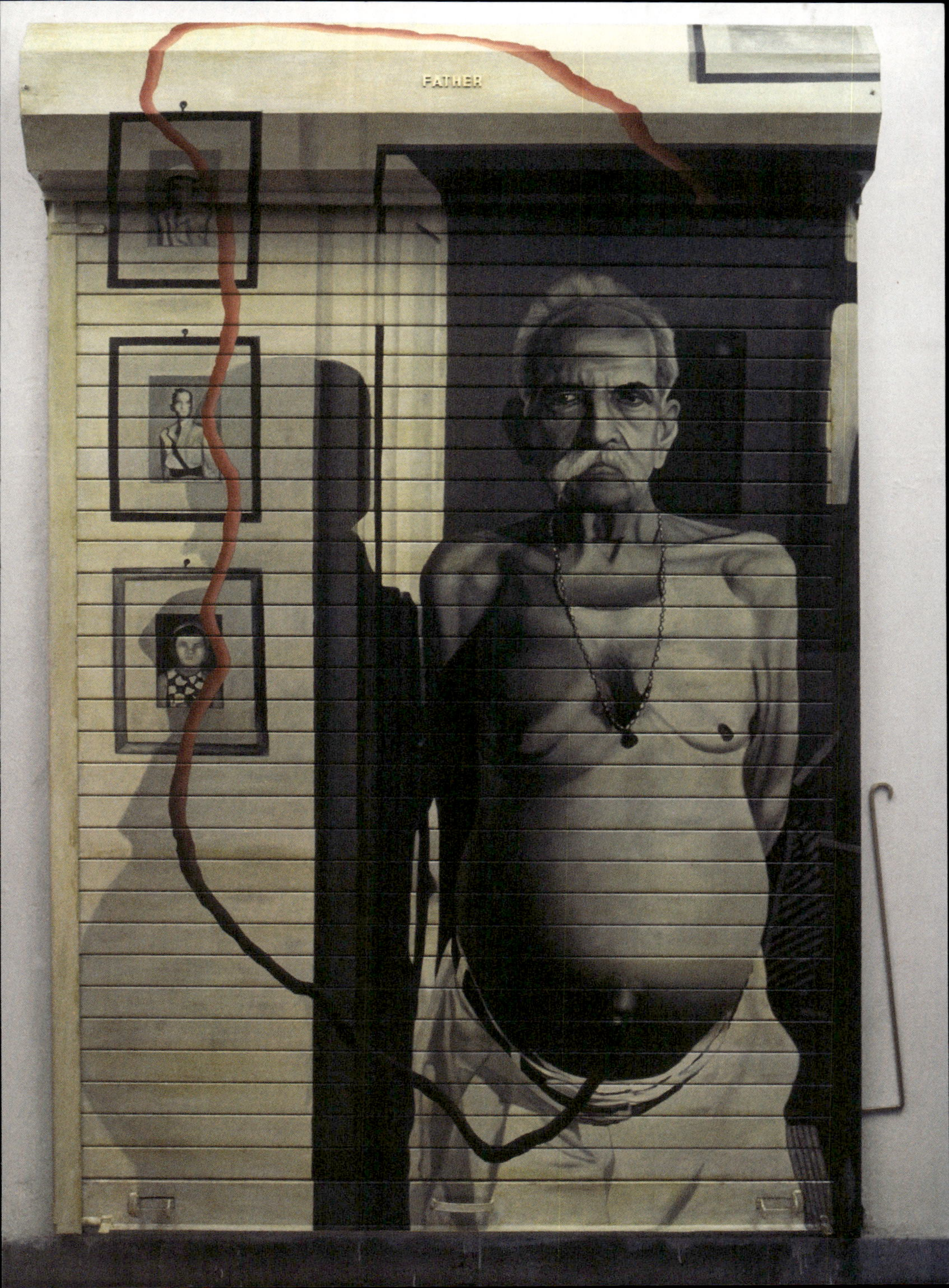
FATHER

4.

The journalist Ravish Kumar made a post on Facebook about a book he was reading. Ashok Lavasa, a top bureaucrat, the head of the national election commission in India, had written a book about his father. The book was titled *An Ordinary Life*. Ravish's post asked, what was it that made ordinary lives worth telling? Lavasa's book hadn't engaged in any name-dropping, it had no stories of decisive moments in a nation's life and his own role in them; it only offered stories about his father, stories that had passed unnoticed by all. An example presented by Ravish in his Facebook post: The father is standing at a railway platform with his young son, the author of the book, who is only nine years old. The father is anxious because his other child, his thirteen-year-old daughter, has been admitted to the local hospital. She is suffering from pneumonia and her life is in danger. The boy is to be dropped off in another town at a boarding house; that is the reason why they are at the railway station. The father resolves his dilemma by asking a stranger, a fellow passenger on the train, if he will please take the child to the boarding house. The stranger says yes and the father rushes back to the daughter. The boy who grows up to become the head of the election commission is telling the story of his father's faith in humanity. This is one meaning of an ordinary life. I copied down this post and read it over and over again. I was thinking about my own father. Even if you come from a poor background and have led a life of limited means, do you not deserve a story of your own?

The privilege of writing a novel is that you make up things. I borrowed from my father's life—his birth in a village in Champaran, his life in nearby Motihari which has the distinction of being George Orwell's birthplace, his interest in writing history—but I was inventing details on every page. Did my father have a crush on Madhubala, a popular Bollywood actress of the 1950s? In a playful gesture, would a man like my father be given a gift two or three decades later, a wallet with a picture of that actress printed on it? I certainly thought it possible and put the picture of such a wallet in my novel. The wallet was real but because the circumstances described in the novel were imagined, I felt I was smuggling contraband in from the realm of the actual.

5.

In the summer of 2021, I heard the novelist Claire Messud read out an essay at a workshop where we were both teaching; in the essay, Messud described her father drawing on a piece of paper a map of his native Beirut. He was drawing the map from memory; a perfectly accurate map of a city where he had grown up but not visited for decades. At that time, I was midway through writing *My Beloved Life*, and I came back that night to my hotel room and made a drawing of my ancestral village. As the months passed, the drawing led me to new thoughts. (I'm telling you this because I want to explain this process—visual prompt leading to narrative discoveries.) I had discovered a story about a teacher in Georgia, who, when his memory began to slip away, started drawing fantastically accurate maps of the route he took to his school and of other places that were a part of his routine. As my story evolved, I also had the father in my story drawing a map of his village. The father in my story has one child, a daughter, and she notices that the map her father has drawn is only of the village as it was during his childhood. Her father hasn't included any of the places that have come up and changed during his daughter's lifetime. A map of a remembered village. It is an accurate map but an outdated one.

6.

It was important that the story of the teacher who drew maps was from a place near Atlanta. I liked this because Jugnu, the daughter in *My Beloved Life,* lived in that city and worked as a journalist for CNN. In trying to imagine the stories this journalist would cover, I found other images. For example, a photograph of Rev. Martin Luther King Jr. visiting the Gandhi Memorial on his visit to India. The detail that had caught the photographer's eye in the photo showed the reverend removing his shoes before walking on to the Gandhi Memorial at Rajghat. (MLK had said: 'To other nations I might go as a tourist. To India I go as a pilgrim.') It was an unconventional image, a distinguished foreign visitor taking off his shoes out of respect for local custom. How would

Indians of different generations respond to this? I wanted to use the MLK photo to show my characters' attitudes.

I also found out that at least two dozen Black children were murdered between 1979 and 1981 in Atlanta, and that James Baldwin had written a journalistic report about these murders that was published as a book in 1985, *The Evidence of Things Not Seen*. In his report, Baldwin had focused not so much on the deaths as on the conditions of the murdered kids' lives. While researching Baldwin's writings, I came across an essay by Robert Reid-Pharr in the *Berlin Journal* that described a teacher's memory of the young Baldwin in high school. The teacher had asked his pupils to step up to the blackboard and describe a scene from nature. Baldwin chose a winter scene and wrote on the board about 'the houses in their little white overcoats'. The image was so striking that when I read it, I thought I should immediately make a drawing. But, dear reader, of all the images I have presented you so far, images that were a part of the thinking about the novel and writing it, how many of these images do you think made it to the final version of the book? Please go on reading to find the answer.

7.

Dodiya's painting of the aged father, his body connected to a tube, had given me a sense of focus. I could imagine a man dying. The painting provided direction to my writing as I imagined an old man on his deathbed during the pandemic. The images, particularly the one of the film actress Madhubala, were ways for me to introduce an element of whimsical play into the story that I was telling. However, to be honest, I was unsure about the rest of the images. I didn't have the kind of conviction I had possessed when I had put my painting of

Mohammed Naeem's lynching in my last novel. My editors in the US and in Canada politely but quite clearly suggested that they were not convinced that an honest narration of stories about ordinary lives needed the distraction of pictures. I hesitated a little bit but this was only because in any other context I would have argued that images, deployed in the right manner, open up a reflective space for the reader. But I quickly made up my mind and deleted all the images you have seen so far.

The only image that is present in *My Beloved Life* is that of a screengrab I had taken. A journalist in Lucknow had tweeted about his falling oxygen level. He had repeatedly appealed for help but none came. His last tweet was sent when his oxygen level was down to thirty-one. Then, nothing.

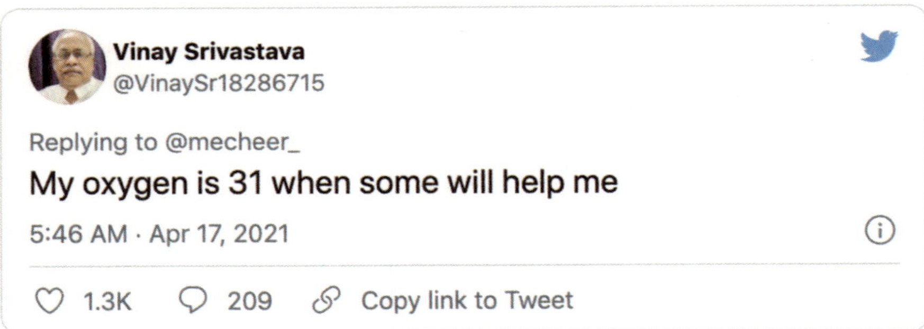

I had gone back to facts. In the face of the Indian government's assertion that it had done everything it could to fight the pandemic and that there was enough oxygen for all who needed it, I felt I needed to tell the truth even though my book was fiction. Fiction because my character reads the tweet and calls her boss at CNN, Roberta, and Roberta tells her that

Christiane Amanpour was in London and it was likely that she would catch a flight to Delhi. Would Amanpour really be going to India to report on the second wave of COVID? It appeared unlikely. My character has this realization in her head:

While Roberta was talking, I could suddenly see Amanpour standing on a boat on the Ganga, the burning pyres of Varanasi behind her, the posh accent delivering news about the fresh 200,000 cases of coronavirus in the country.

Instead of Amanpour, it is my co-protagonist who goes. All of this started with the above tweet that I had read, in real time, by the doomed journalist Vinay Srivastava. In using the image of his tweet I was trying to report on an ordinary life and what sadly for many was an ordinary death.

Green, an Unripe Time

It is dusk, or call it middle age, the grass
is the colour of forever, and I wait for the
children to never stop running toward me.

The picture that you see here was taken a decade ago by the writer Hua Hsu at a wedding in upstate New York. I stand now at the cusp of old age, the twilight years, my gaze turned toward the gathering dark that lyrical writers call the gloaming. But for a brief moment, I want to consider not the immediate future but the more distant and irrecoverable past.

I have in my files a drawing made for my twenty-first birthday by a girl I was in love with. By being in love I don't mean that we had ever kissed or even held hands; we would run into each other at college in Delhi and make small talk for a minute or two but then we often wrote each other long, intense letters. A few times I visited her at home for tea, and on one memorable occasion, she came to my home for lunch and met my mother. On a visit to Patna a few years ago, I found my decades-old journals in my parents' home. Secreted in their pages were all the letters from her that I had saved.

Her drawing was part of a letter I must have received in 1984. I never drew her, I wouldn't have known how to. On the campus of my college, where I seldom attended class, my eyes always searched for her. I don't know why our conversations were so brief, even abrupt; I was always nervous when I saw her and my mouth would go dry. I was elated when I received her letters. Often I waited for them in vain, and I experienced an emptiness, a quiet nullity of being, when days passed without letters. I thought of all this when some time ago I read the following line by Oscar Wilde: 'What was youth at best? A green, an unripe time, a time of shallow moods and sickly thoughts.'

When I came across those words from Wilde, I was working on the novel that became *My Beloved Life*. One of my two protagonists is a young woman named Jugnu who is studying journalism at a college in Delhi. She exchanges letters with a fellow student named Jatin. The letters that Jatin writes aren't conventional letters: they only have a line or two quoted from a book he is reading. He doesn't mention the author or the title of the book the quote has been borrowed from. This makes Jugnu feel cheated; she complains, because she wants to further her education. These details in the novel are not autobiographical.

In the novel, I put these words which feel true even now: 'When passing a cup of coffee, or when exchanging books or even letters, my fingers brushed against Jatin's hands. But there was no other intimacy.' Jatin believes that his true calling is to be a poet but his poems are full of vague abstractions.

When I found the letters in my old diaries, I also discovered a rejection letter that had been sent to me by an editor. I put that letter in my novel, hardly changed, as an accidental discovery by Jugnu. She reads it with a sense of guilt and embarrassment, and then wonders if Jatin had wanted her to find it and offer him sympathy.

Opposite:
Green mountains,
Vermont, 2023

Dear Jatin,
You do show potential for good poetry, but only if you realize that you suffer from one major flaw that seems to have gripped modern poetry everywhere—a lot of words and little meaning. The poems do make interesting reading, because words have their own peculiar beauty—but because of a deliberate obscurity or a confusion of ideas and images, these poems have no lasting value, nor do they have any depth of feeling or thought…

That is where Jugnu stops reading the letter. She folds it and puts it back in the book of Freud's selected writings where she had found it.

When you are young and inexperienced, you are awkward and don't know how to conduct yourself in love. You also don't know how to make art. You might have taste but you have zero accomplishments. However, and this is the important thing, it is precisely your good taste that makes you feel disappointed in your work, as the radio host Ira Glass once put it. It is 'only by going through a volume of work,' Glass says, 'you will close that gap and your work will be as good as your ambitions.'

Opposite:
Green mountains,
orange tractor,
Vermont, 2023

I brought the packet of letters back to the United States with me from Patna and left them untouched for three or four years. When I tried to read them, I found it a dismal experience. I could hardly recognize the person I had once been.

Then, during the summer two years ago, I returned to the letters. They were spotted with age, and the pins and clips holding them together were rusted. This was true also of the rejection letter sent by the editor of the magazine. What had changed was that there was now a shelf full of the books I had written. Occasionally, I think of the girl I knew at twenty-one (does she draw still?) and silently wish her well.

Opposite:
Geometry,
Vermont, 2023

Modern Indian History, 2024

Saffron and Green

I was born and grew up in India and I'm trying to remember when I became Indian.

In the summer of 1986, a police constable on a bicycle came to my home in the city of Patna to conduct an inquiry. This visit was in response to my application for a passport. Two weeks later my passport was ready. I was twenty-three years old, preparing to go to the United States to attend a graduate programme in literature. Did I first become Indian when I acquired my passport?

If so, it would be paradoxical that I became Indian at the very moment I was most eager to get away from India.

But there must have been earlier occasions.

I was eight when Bangladesh was liberated with the help of the Indian army in December 1971. I had a vague sense that the Indian armed forces and Prime Minister Indira Gandhi had defeated the Pakistanis, and they had also outfoxed the rotund man with thick glasses in newspaper photographs, Henry Kissinger. Maybe it was then that I adopted my nascent national identity?

When I was a little older, my father's job took us to Bokaro, a city where the Russians had helped build a steel factory. One day I met the Russian engineers and their families at an event where they were giving out gifts, including pins with Vladimir Lenin's head embossed on them. This first real encounter with foreigners, maybe that was the day when I thought of myself as Indian?

I'm forgetting something.

From my early childhood, my family would travel from our ancestral village in Champaran to a nearby town across the border in Nepal. This was in pre-liberalization India, when our markets were closed to foreign products. In Nepal, we could buy Chinese and Japanese products. For our trip back, women hid new chiffon sarees under their garments. In my pockets, I would have anything from a new transistor radio to a sleek camera or just a pack of peppermint-flavoured Wrigley's gum. My first typewriter, a red portable Brother, was bought during one of these trips not long after I had entered college.

Passports were not required during these visits to Nepal. The cycle-rickshaws we hired trundled past the customs crossing without rigorous checks. But what I want to say is that the knowledge that I was breaking the law (smuggling!) weighed on me more than the issue of national difference.

Now that I think about it, a sense of a self and the idea of this self also inhabiting a particular place, a place as large as a country, only came to me when I saw the outlines of a national literature, that is, when I had grasped the notion of a body of literature that told our stories. In other words, sometime during my late teens I became Indian because I had acquired a complex language—a gift given by writers who had come before me—that described the people and places around me.

I admired the grasp that Khushwant Singh, Dom Moraes, Anita Desai, Nayantara Sahgal, Ved Mehta and a young Salman Rushdie had on a broad but also intimate language that established them as Indian, one that embraced history, landscape, people and their mixed identities. Singh's 1956 novel *A Train to Pakistan* in particular was instructive about the history of Hindus, Muslims and Sikhs having lived together peaceably, and then, caught in the maelstrom of history, transforming into each other's murderers. Even V.S. Naipaul, born in distant Trinidad, was Indian because he had so accurately, if testily, depicted the spaces in which was staged the drama of our large and untidy collective identity.

I should clarify that I wasn't at all fluent in that language myself. In fact, I felt quite inadequate. In the 1980s, when I entered my twenties, India saw riots, a huge industrial disaster in Bhopal, and the assassination of Indira Gandhi and the killings of Sikhs that followed it. But it was as if I was looking at these events standing mutely behind a thick glass. More years would pass before I could employ a vocabulary to communicate in that language of national belonging and translate that trauma onto the page in the hopes of a reckoning.

By the time a Hindu mob destroyed the old mosque in the city of Ayodhya on 6 December 1992, I was ready to speak out. I recognized that a planned effort by an organized, ultranationalist party had unleashed the demon of hatred in Indian society. I was finishing my doctoral studies at the time and saw zealots from my own Hindu community in the United States donating gold bricks for the construction of a temple on the disputed site. In the books I wrote over the ensuing decade, *Passport Photos* and then *Bombay-London-New York*, I argued that in the Indian diaspora the soft emotion of nostalgia had been turned into the hard emotion of fundamentalism.

In the early 1990s, I was also training to be a scholar of postcolonial literature—a term describing, for the most part, the literature of countries in Africa and Asia that had achieved freedom from colonialism. My peers included people from Ethiopia, Ireland, South Africa, Sri Lanka and Pakistan. When we read, say, Rushdie or Jamaica Kincaid, Nadine Gordimer or Ngugi wa Thiong'o, Edward Said or Nawal el Saadawi, we were focusing on critiques of colonialism and its lingering history.

The freedom struggles of our own countries had been carried out under the flag of nationalism. But decades after Independence, it was difficult to ignore the actions of our own governments run by the privileged and the powerful. We faulted our own postcolonial states for having produced parodies of nationalism.

But this led to a peculiar problem. If one said anything negative about India, for instance, one invited the charge of representing the 'colonial mindset'. There was the criticism of writing in English, also that of living abroad. All variety of narrow nationalists accused my field of postcolonial studies of being inauthentic, a prisoner of the Western mentality that had traditionally looked down upon the countries of the East. This situation was rich with irony.

In 2002, riots in the state of Gujarat killed, by official count, 790 Muslims and 254 Hindus, though unofficial estimates

Figures on a stage, 2023

place the death toll at 2,000. The chief minister of Gujarat at that time was Narendra Modi, and his party, the BJP, was also in power in Delhi. In the aftermath of the riots, I reported from Ahmedabad's relief camps for Muslim refugees and carried on my investigations into religious violence elsewhere, including in various parts of Kashmir. My writings earned me a place on a 'hit-list' run by Hindu ultranationalists in the United States, and BJP supporters accused me of being anti-Hindu and anti-India. India's right wing saw me as a foreigner.

The Nobel Prize-winning poet Rabindranath Tagore, a part

of whose song '*Bharoto Bhagyo Bidhata*' was adopted as India's national anthem, wrote in 1917 that 'nationalism is a great menace'.

Tagore was warning us against what he called 'social slavery' that 'impels us to make the life of our fellow-beings a burden to them where they differ from us even in such a thing as their choice of food.' A century after Tagore wrote his essay, his words appear like a grim prophecy when mobs have lynched Muslims in different parts of India on the suspicion of eating beef. (In 2014, Hindutva supporters said they'd send prominent writer U.R. Ananthamurthy a ticket to Pakistan when he expressed strong opposition to the election of Modi and the BJP that year. The Hindu ultranationalists would like to send to Pakistan—alongside a lot of India's Muslims—all those Indian citizens who dare dissent and whom they call "anti-nationals".)

The inauguration of the Ram temple at the site of the demolished mosque in Ayodhya in 2024, with the prime minister administering the rites and with many prominent citizens present, achieved the Hindutva goal of deifying the Indian nationalist identity as Hindu. The frenzied state-aided celebrations, the kowtowing in the media, the establishment of a mythical history as a near-constitutional fact, put the seal of majoritarianism on everyday life.

The recent events represent the culmination of a process that has upended all that was meant by 'postcolonial'. For me and many others, to be postcolonial was to share a sense of historical kinship with others who had suffered under the lash of colonialism. Chinua Achebe spoke to us, and Kincaid was recognizable to us, because they were witnesses to what our countries too had experienced. To be postcolonial also entailed the right to critique our current regimes, because our tainted present wasn't what we had been promised, and this required a fight for greater equality and the rule of law. Yet the Hindutva brigade no longer talks of British rule as colonial conquest. Instead, for them, it is the arrival of Mughal armies 500 years ago, and the Islamic dynasty they established, that signals the onset of colonialism.

This is a cunning strategy on the part of the ruling party and its increasing ranks of faithful followers. By painting the Muslim as the enemy, the Hindu right succeeds in consolidating the Hindu vote across caste and class lines, all unified in opposition to ever-more marginalized minorities. Prices, unemployment and economic inequality are all rising, but we need not address those problems because we are told that our difficulties have to do with a minority that constitutes 14.2 per cent of India's population. The colour green, associated with Islam, and, as it happens, one of the three colours on the tiranga, the Indian national flag, has become suspect. Saffron is now seemingly the only colour that enjoys acceptance.

Am I an Indian? Yes, if it means finding the common cause of freedom across religious lines. No, if it means the idolatry of a nation built around a singular religious identity and the cult worship of a single leader.

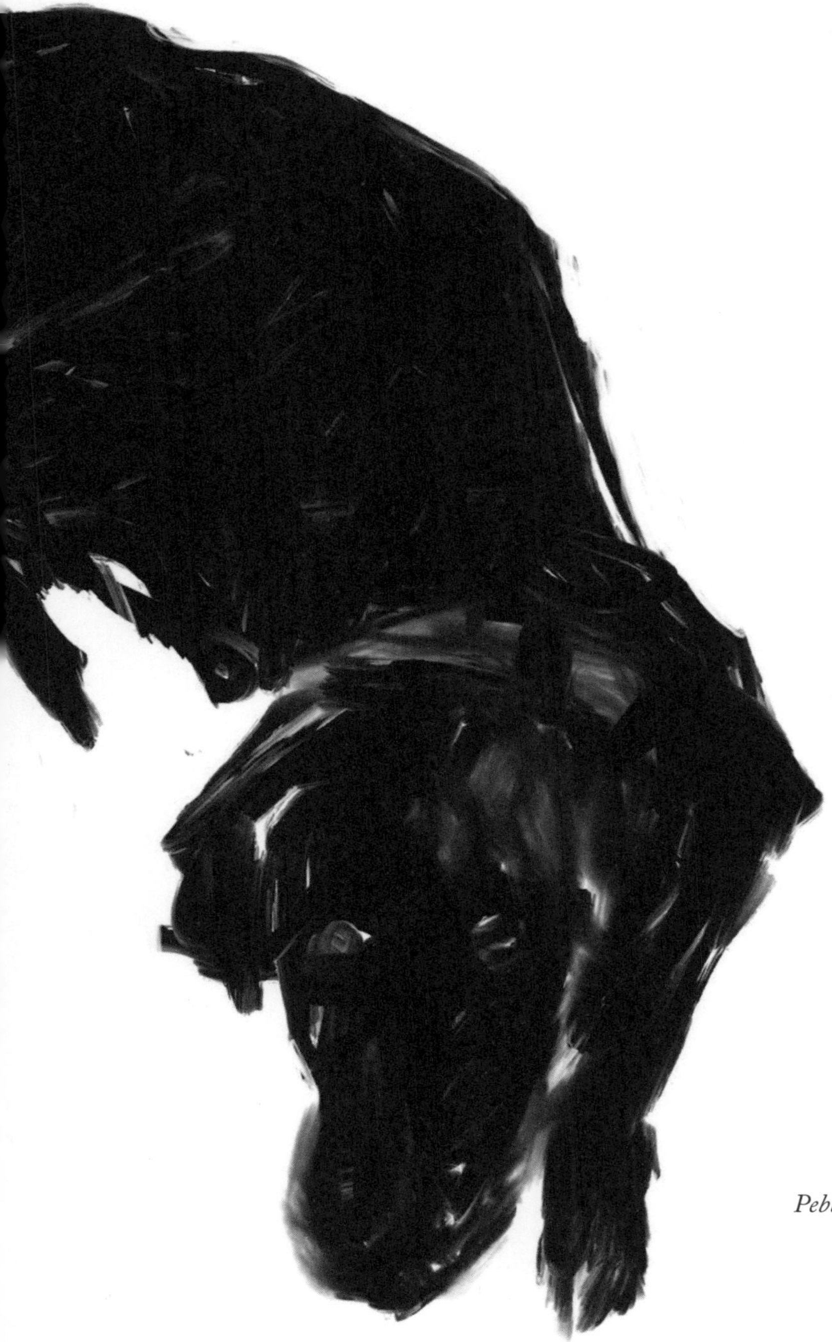

Pebble, Fairfax, 2023

All That Breathes

The first creature that we see in the documentary film *All That Breathes* is a dog. A street dog dimly visible in the crepuscular squalor of urban decay. We are in a corner of Hamdard Chowk in Old Delhi. We see the dog but what we hear is the sound of scurrying, screeching rats. So many rats. After four minutes, the screen turns white, as if catching the light of a passing car, and the name of the film appears. *All That Breathes*.

Only then does the ostensible subject of the film appear, a kite high in the sky, floating lazily on a current of air. The voice that speaks is that of one of the brothers who form the main cast: the men who save birds that are brought to them in their basement in Delhi. We hear the voice say: 'When other birds fly, their effort shows. But the kite swims ...' Then, there is a cut and we are watching and listening to the hum of mosquitoes in a puddle where, reflected upside down, we also see other creatures, including humans and goats. This is an important aspect of this remarkable documentary: *All That Breathes* is ostensibly about birds and the brothers who care for them but what it is really about is an attentiveness to all living beings. When I spoke about this with him over lunch in Delhi, the film's director Shaunak Sen reached for a phrase made popular by the evolutionary biologist Lyn Margulis who wrote about 'the intimacy of strangers'. She conducted research that showed that living entities form hybrid or composite life forms in order to produce the conditions for collective flourishing. Sen told me that 'human exceptionalism is obsolete in every sense of the word' and 'entanglement or neighbourliness' is life's fundamental fact. In many ways, *All That Breathes* is an exploration of this belief. Later, in another passage presented as a voice-over, one of the brothers says: 'You don't care for things because they share with you the same country, religion, or politics. Life itself is kinship. We are all a community of air. That's why we can't abandon the birds. More and more fall from the sky every day ...'

Life in a modern urban space is a fight for survival, it is the generosity of strangers, it is jugaad. So much of the care for the hurt birds takes place in a shabby, dimly-lit basement which is also partly a workshop and partly a garage. In one frame, a pillar dissects one half of the basement space where, on the right, a man is sitting at a desk working with a screwdriver in his hand; in the area to the left, the young cousin of the two brothers is examining a kite's damaged wings. The film is a paean to gritty city life, its horrors—a tender elegy, really—but also to the evolution of new modes of endurance. As the camera lingers over birds sitting or flying above chimneys and between long loops of electric wires and pylons, we hear a voice reporting on how nature has been transformed: 'As Delhi's air changed, so did its metabolism. Song-birds sing at a higher pitch, to communicate over traffic noise. Lizards are growing new toes. The kite is a traditional bird. A kite rests, roosts, bathes and attacks in the same style—all its life. Every kite has a code—but code-breaking has become natural today. Every life form adjusts to the city now. Rats, pigs, frogs, mosquitoes, turtles, insects, cows and horses ... All improvise and adapt to the city.' The urban kites are more innovative than rural kites. The brothers report finding cigarette butts in the caged enclosures for the kites. The understanding dawned on them that the birds were using the cigarette butts as parasite repellants. The human is now a part of the natural environment of the city birds. Even evolution, in other words, has recognized the truth of the entanglement that Sen was telling me about.

As the film's viewers we might wonder why the brothers do what they do? A part of the explanation comes again in a voice-over. We are watching a kite floating in the sky near the pale outline of the moon in the daytime sky. Then we witness a man on the top of the steps throwing into the air what must be pieces of meat as the birds wheel and swoop above him. We hear the voice say: 'It's said that feeding kites earns "sawab" (religious credit). When they eat the meat you offer, they eat away your difficulties. And their hunger is insatiable ...' But this is only a part of the story. The brothers were body-builders when they were teens; that is how they got an understanding of flesh, muscles and tendon. While running a business making soap dispensers, they started saving kites. The local bird hospital didn't accept kites because these birds ate meat. (Charity was only for the vegetarian birds!) So the brothers read *Muscle Flex* and started treating the injured kites. There is a similar this-worldliness in the treatment of the question of the limitations that the brothers face in their work: power cuts, lack of funding, machines that stop working, the incessant heat, more deaths of the birds.

'Man is the loneliest animal,' the younger brother says in a voice-over as we watch people gathered on rooftops to fly the other kind of kites, the paper ones. He goes on: 'Trapped by this speciestic difference. It's like a jail.' What is the way out of this prison? We find out in the very next sequence. Both brothers, wearing skullcaps, are praying beside a grave in a cemetery in Old Delhi. The grave is their mother's; she died of cancer. The brothers look up when they hear a bird's call. One of them says, 'Spotted owlet.' In yet another remarkable voice-over we learn that it is their mother who drew them to animals and science by telling stories about ghosts and holy spirits. Their mother's mantra provides the film's title: 'One shouldn't differentiate between all that breathes.' A credo for the anthropocene! We are living at a time when 30,000 species per year are being driven to extinction. This means we are making eighty-two species extinct every day.

All That Breathes is attentive to all forms of life—a turtle climbing over a pile of rubbish, a snail crawling near a fire, a lizard on the wall, pigs rooting in a nullah—and it also reminds us that we must also attend to humans. This reminder is a more subtle intervention in the course of the film. As we get deeper into the film, we are told that we cannot divide and differentiate among our fellow humans.

There is a famous psychological experiment conducted by Harvard scientists sometimes called 'the invisible gorilla'. The participants in the test are asked to watch a screen on which can be seen six people (three in white, and three in black) passing two basketballs around. The given task is to keep a silent count of the number of passes made by the group in white. While this is going on in a tight space, a figure in a gorilla suit walks into the frame, thumps its chest when standing in the middle, and then walks off the other end after spending nine seconds on the screen. The gorilla when thus described seems an obvious thing to notice, but when the study was conducted several years ago, the researchers found that half of the people who watched the video and counted the passes made by the people in white completely missed the gorilla. The experiment is offered as proof of our selective attentiveness. I mention this experiment because *All That*

Breathes both uses and demonstrates what 'the invisible gorilla' reveals. We have been so focused on the birds and perhaps the other non-human creatures that we do not immediately notice that in the background can be heard the slogans of protest. These sounds on the public address system are coming from a place very close to where the brothers live. In the beginning, the brothers don't pay attention to this and we don't either. The protests are against the government's proposals for constitutional changes in citizenship laws that were widely perceived as being discriminatory against Muslims. We are half an hour into the film when the subject is introduced directly into conversation. It is a part of a conversation around a family dinner: the brothers and their wives are talking about being turned into refugees. The subject is thought-provoking but the manner is nearly light-hearted. There is a cut and the brothers are dealing with something more immediate, rising waters and flooding in the lane outside due to rainfall. We then see how the basement floor is covered with rainwater. And this scene is taken over by concerns about funding. There are enough distractions, if that is the word I want, to draw our attention to other matters. And then, we return in a new, urgent way to what is happening outside. The Muslim neighbourhood is going up in flames.

Half an hour before the film comes to an end, the wife of one of the brothers has returned from the protest. Gently but with a quiet urgency, she urges her husband to visit the protest site at least once. Like us, he is preoccupied with the kites—and he doesn't see the gorilla. But the camera is paying attention, it gathers fleeting footage and picks up sounds even if from a distance. (I enjoyed this aesthetic strategy immensely and when I told Sen about this, he said, 'Films that reveal their political cards too easily—too early—are actually apolitical.') The birds are falling from the sky, the fridge where the meat for the kites is stored breaks down, many of the birds are dying, their fledglings need to be cared for and the dead ones need to be buried. There is always so much to do. When violence arrives, we don't see it. We only hear it as the young cousin of the brothers, who has been assisting them, gets a call from his worried mother. We can see him, as he travels in a three-wheeler, watching footage of the rioting on his phone. He keeps the phone away and after a minute takes out a baby squirrel from his shirt's pocket and plays with the tiny creature. This is another great feature of *All That Breathes*: if you are going to really pay attention to all that is life, time has to be slowed down and your narrative has to possess a durational intensity. This pattern remains in this section toward the end of the film. There is news of horrific violence in the riots—this was in February 2020—but while we hear what the TV anchors are saying, the footage that we are watching is only of different creatures, horses, ants, a camel, kites, an owl.

In the film's last fifteen minutes, we are back with the birds. The brothers have built their new hospital. Working through the day and night, they transfer 172 birds into the new structure. They watch the healthy kites sail out of their cage. It is then that we hear one of the brothers say the words that I had cited at the beginning of this piece and which we should remember, like a prayer, each day of the anthropocene: 'You don't care for things because they share with you the same country, religion, or politics. Life itself is kinship. We are all a community of air.'

Ray
Ami

Opposite page:
Ray and Otis, Rhinebeck and Poughkeepsie, 2022
Pebble, Chicago, 2022

This page:
Jasper, Toronto, 2022
Pebble Dibu, 2022

Overleaf:
Gabby, Millbrook, 2023
Louise, New York City, 2022

GO, GET THE MINT, GABBY!

Prison Green

During the Spring semester in 2023, I got the chance to teach a literature course in the nearby Fishkill Correctional Facility. I had six male students and the course I was teaching was at an advanced bachelor's level. During the orientation meeting before I started teaching, I learned two things that interested me: first, inmates who graduated from the bachelor's programme were unlikely to fall foul of the law and return to prison; and second, the prison staff resented the fact that the inmates, who in their eyes were criminals, were receiving a free education. My supervisor also told me that I was to leave everything in my car and that I should step inside with nothing but my car keys, the pre-approved syllabus and reading material, and a sealed purchased bottle of water. No cell phones, no laptops, no books or paper that hadn't been vetted before, no wallet. And I wasn't to wear green because that was the colour of the uniform worn by the prison inmates. It goes without saying then that any drawing I made in my class was done on any empty page in the photocopied textbook we were using; I felt not just shy but also wrong drawing my students on the sly but a part of me also felt that in drawing them, and now in writing about them, I was also maybe giving them a solidity that the state denied them.

I would arrive at the prison and drive past the first gate after showing my driver's license and explaining my purpose. After I had parked I would go up the steps and a guard would open the first set of double doors. My information first needed to be entered in a logbook. The guard then took my own ID and gave me the prison ID which worked internally; I was scanned with a metal detector and my hand stamped with invisible ink. What followed was a long period of waiting in a nearby corridor. The wait was for a corrections officer from

Student, Fishkill, 2023

inside who would escort me to my classroom. On occasion, if there was a fight inside or any other kind of disturbance, I might need to wait for an hour. When the officer arrived, we would go through more locked doors and then undergo another check by a guard on the inside.

On the walk to my classroom, beyond the glinting barbed wire and the tall electric fences to my right, I could see the interstate highway and in the far distance green mountains.

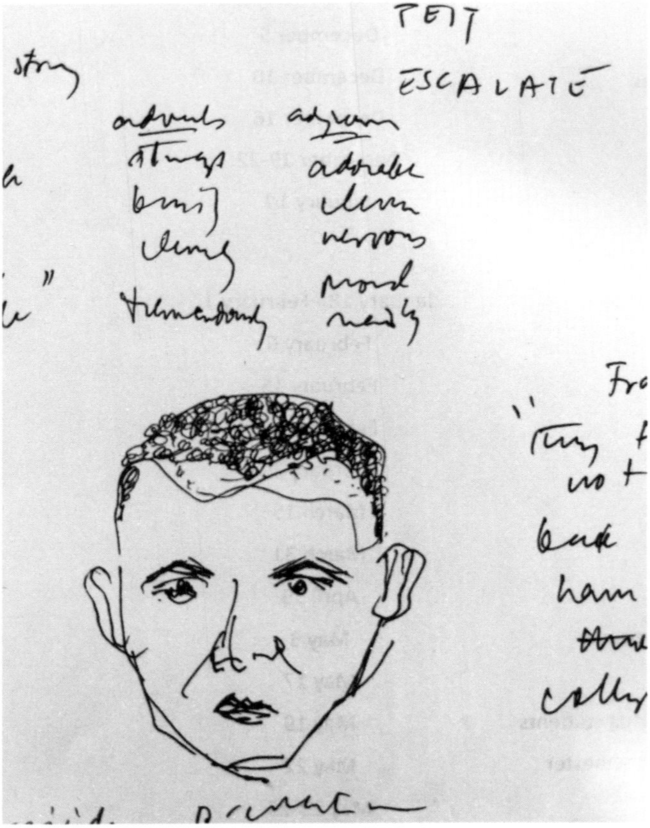

Student,
Fishkill, 2023

While I walked, the guard and I made small talk; on the other side of the road, a long row of prisoners in green would be walking in the opposite direction, headed to various parts of the prison, the mess hall, the infirmary, the carpentry room, the confectionary, etc. I never got the chance to speak to any inmate who wasn't my student. I had been advised during orientation to not engage in any loose conversation with my fellow teachers from other institutions and to never address my students by their first names. It was emphasized that I wasn't to make any personal conversation with the inmates in my class and also that I wasn't to inquire about the nature of the crime that had brought them to Fishkill.

The course I was teaching was called 'Literature from Elsewhere'. The books we read included Jamaica Kincaid's *A Small Place*, Mohsin Hamid's *Exit, West*, Zadie Smith's *The Embassy of Cambodia* and Valeria Luiselli's *Tell Me How It Ends: An Essay in 40 Questions*. We met for a couple of hours each week. You would think that there would be a lot of time in prison but what I discovered was that 'doing time' is an apt phrase because it means that you must surrender your hours and minutes, resigning yourself to a blankness. But surrender to whom? Not necessarily to an individual, or never merely to an individual. Time as controlled by a faceless, distant, opaque and cruel system of nearly arbitrary rules. My students did their best to do the readings and were also often diligent about submitting written responses. Whether we were reading about a Mexican child on the US border or an immigrant woman widowed in Manchester, I wanted us to get a sense of contemporary globalization. In almost each of our readings we were reminded about how structures of power shape not only how people move, or get moved, around the world, but also how books move and get moved around the global literary space. It was my hope that one day when my students were released and would step out into freedom, they would have an insight into the vast currents governing the world. And, in a more immediate sense, while they stayed behind the prison walls, it was my hope that they were gathering an enriching experience of the vast world outside that was denied them during their incarceration.

Student, Fishkill, 2023

My students in the prison class needed no lessons in the workings of power, of course. What I wanted for the readings we were doing in class to offer them was a more systemic or structural view of power in a global frame. I didn't teach prison literature, although there was one short story by Chimamanda Ngozi Adichie that dealt with that theme; what I was really trying to do was present for discussion scenes from life in which my students recognized themselves. Above all, I wanted them to feel less alone.

One student, whom I'll call Scott, began to write about a fight on a street among two groups of teenagers. It was late night, tempers were frayed. After being surprised by a punch to his mouth when trying to separate two boys who were fighting, a third boy, the one who had been punched in the mouth, pulled out a knife. In a flash, the fight was over. The boy with the knife had drawn blood. Later, sitting at home with his family in front of the television the next evening, he would learn that the boy who had been knifed had died in the hospital. Now, for the boy with the knife, the wait began for the police to arrive at his door.

In Scott's essay, the scene shifted to the courtroom. On one side sat the family that was grieving because they had lost a son. On the other side the narrator's family because they were also losing their son who was going to spend the next twenty-five years in prison. (I had learned from somewhere that Scott had said that he had already been in prison for twenty years.) It was a tragedy for both families and Scott had written in his essay that 'finding the right words are never easy' to describe the complexity of a scene like that. When I read those words,

I realized that what we were trying to do in our class was exactly that, we were struggling to find expression, sorting out words to describe as accurately and honestly as we could the condition of the world and our place in it.

Another student, whom I'll call Troy, wrote a short story about a corrections officer at home. The story described the officer's routine work, its rigid demands, and the inevitable degradation. The officer's wife held the work that he did in seeming contempt. The narrator, presenting the story from the correction officer's point of view, said that he was not like the violent men inside the prison who fought without provocation. 'Well, except for that one time. Oh, and there was that other time. And those couple of times when he first started out. And the other day when ...' That is how the story ended. I felt it was very well done. But the most cutting observation in the story had come earlier in the following observation regarding the correction officer's duties from the viewpoint of the inmate: 'He didn't think of the fact that, while he could walk around the entire jail, he was still restricted by the same razor-topped fences as us. His cell was only bigger.'

Very good, I wrote in the margin. Then, after class, I drew Troy aside and asked him if he wanted me to submit the story to a magazine. He said no. He didn't want trouble when his case came up for parole, or even earlier than that at the prison. Art had given Troy the freedom to explore and express his thoughts, but there was no use pretending that this freedom was without real constraints.

And yet, I liked how in so much of the work they did in my

class, the students were always drawing the lines. Or pointing to the lines that divided one section of society from another. To quote one example, here is an exchange recorded by a student I will call Terrell:

> 'It's not fair that I have to use my tax dollars to pay for a prisoner's education,' says the corrections officer.
> 'If it weren't for prisoners, you wouldn't have a job and wouldn't be able to pay for your kids' college education,' I said.

We were never far from approaching or understanding and portraying conflict in that class. It was a valuable experience, not least because it let us believe that education would redeem you, and that reading or writing was a shared activity that enhanced our humanity. If you didn't consign individuals to the trash bin, there was hope. Flowers would bloom where there had been parched earth.

Coda: One day toward the end of the semester, with summer now upon us, Scott brought a Labrador puppy to class. Dogs were being trained in the prison system and inmates could apply to be allowed to keep a pet. The puppy was soon going to be given to Scott. He was a well-behaved animal. He played for a while and then as the lesson went on, he fell asleep on the floor. Such unexpected joy. Only once before had we been surprised by this feeling of sudden happiness in class. We were discussing a short story by Petina Gappah titled 'The Mupandawana Dancing Champion'. We had come across a description of the protagonist, an old man who is a coffin maker, stunning the dancers at a competition with his prowess. What followed was a list of dance moves: 'He knew all the latest dances, and those before the latest. We gaped at his reebok and his water pump. He stunned us with his running man. He killed us with his robot. And his snake dance and his break dance made us stand and say ho-o. His moonwalk made Michael himself stand and say ho-o ...' This went on for a while but I had to stop. I asked the class if anyone knew, for example, the running man. I had looked it up on the Internet the previous night. Each one of the students

Puppy,
Fishkill, 2023

seemed to know the running man. You must remember that we didn't have access to any computers in the classroom, nor any music, of course. But it didn't matter. When I asked if anyone would show me how the dance was done, Terrell said with a puzzled smile, 'You serious?' I nodded. He got up and started slowly and his classmates began to snap their fingers and clap. The sounds they made with their mouths were another kind of music and soon we were going through the names of the other dances that were mentioned in the story. Terrell demonstrated and others followed. I couldn't remain sitting either. For several minutes all of us danced, responding to the rhythm, swaying, stamping to the sound of our fingers and tongues, beginning to now float above the pull of everyday gravity and our walled-off cares.

Nature Writing

Fall, 2022

I have proposed a new course for me to teach at my college. The title I have given the course is 'Nature Writing' but the first title for the course that had come to mind was 'It's Not the Heat, It's the Stupidity'. The latter title would be suitable for a critique of all the wrong-headed policies we have followed as a species. In settling on the more neutral-sounding title, I want to draw attention more to the writing. How have various writers, both in fiction and non-fiction, represented the crisis of climate change and its consequences for all of us and other living beings on Planet Earth?

The point of doing nature writing at this juncture can only be to win converts to the cause. How to save our planet and the fast-vanishing species? In an essay published last year on *The New Yorker* magazine's website, novelist and famous birder Jonathan Franzen wrote that 'the paradox of nature writing is that, to succeed as evangelism, it can't only be about nature'. Most birders, Franzen added, became interested in birds because of 'a parent, a teacher, a close friend, someone they had an intense personal connection with'. This intensity can be rhetorical. Franzen recommends *Ill Nature* by Joy Williams for her 'blistering prose'. Another attraction of nature writing, according to Franzen, can be the presentation of a strong argument. He recommends an essay collection entitled *Tropical Nature* by Adrian Forsyth and Ken Miyata because 'scientific facts speak far more compellingly to the glory of tropical nature than lyrical impressionism' and because the writers are scientists, they, 'as neutral bringers of fact, remain immune to the suspicion of seeking admiration'. Similar recommendations for Jennifer Ackerman's *The Genius of Birds* and Richard Prum's *The Evolution of Beauty.* A third avenue to intensity, Franzen tells us, 'is to tell a story in which the focus is on nature but the dramatic stakes are emphatically human'. The example he gives is Kenn Kaufman's *Kingbird Highway*, an account of an obsessive birder who drops out of high school with the aim of 'breaking the record for the most American bird species seen in a calendar year.' An animal or a bird doesn't have 'the particularity of the self' on which good storytelling depends, and so, 'only a human character will suffice'. Which brings us to Franzen's conclusion: 'We can't make a reader care about nature. All we can do is tell strong stories of people who do care, and hope that the caring is contagious.'

I spoke to Franzen recently, asking him if I should teach the books he had mentioned in my course next semester. He said it would be tricky to name the best examples of any kind of writing with a view to teaching. He explained: 'At the very top you find really extraordinary works that could only have been written by the particular individual … No one else can be Joy Williams.' Kenn Kaufman's *Kingbird Highway* is the best book about birding in Franzen's view, but no one else can write *Kingbird Highway* again. So, teaching any of these books might introduce students to some general precepts about nature, but they cannot be imitated.

I discussed some popular titles and Franzen agreed with me that they ought to be on the list of the course I was going to teach. These were books like Rachel Carson's *Silent Spring* and Elizabeth Kolbert's *The Sixth Extinction*. Franzen said he is a big fan of Dale Jamieson's *Reason in a Dark Time: Why the Struggle Against Climate Change Failed*. He said it had been a 'life-changing book' for him. Jamieson's basic argument is that 'climate crisis is a reflection of human nature; it exists and will not be resolved because of who we are'. I took Franzen to be essentially injecting realism into the debate about climate change by championing this book. He had discussed this book also in a 2015 essay he had written for *The New Yorker*. Four years later, in another essay for the same magazine ('What if We Stopped Pretending'), he had clearly argued that we ought to 'accept that disaster is coming, and begin to rethink what it means to have hope.' The point Franzen was making was that even if climate apocalypse is inevitable, and it is, we should do our best to ensure a few more years of relative stability. Although he was attacked for that essay, the most hopeful, and perhaps meaningful, argument that Franzen presented in that essay was how every ethical thing we did could be interpreted as climate action: 'Any movement toward a more just and civil society can now be considered a meaningful climate action. Securing fair elections is a climate action. Combatting extreme wealth inequality is a climate action. Shutting down the hate machines on social media is a climate action. Instituting humane immigration policy, advocating for racial and gender equality, promoting respect for laws and their enforcement, supporting a free and independent press, ridding the country of assault weapons—these are all meaningful climate actions.'

The above essay where this point is made is perhaps where I would start my course, and then go on to discuss essays from Greta Thunberg's *No One Is Too Small to Make a Difference* and Rebecca Solnit's *Not Too Late*.

Before we ended our conversation, I asked Franzen what he thought of an argument that has been made about novelists not addressing climate change. To Franzen it seemed that every week there is a new book about the subject—it was a bit like the plague of novels after 9/11. He said, 'Should the novelist be the annoying little dog chasing after the garbage truck of history, barking after it has already moved on?' He wanted me to imagine a scenario: even if a made-up thing like the novel completely changed someone's thinking about the future of the planet, what would such a person do? They might start riding a bicycle to work. Franzen said with some emotion: 'It wouldn't make a difference. Even if a million people started riding bicycles as the result of a novel—and here we are in the realm of pure fantasy—it wouldn't make a damned bit of difference.' To require novels to address climate change is a demand, Franzen felt, that is both 'boring and useless'.

But what if we thought of novels in a different way? The writer Lydia Millet made an important point when she told an interviewer that while fiction increasingly studies the 'arc of the private individual', what is more interesting or important is to examine how feelings are 'intermeshed with abstract thought' and 'with our place in the wider landscape'. (No wonder that Millet's latest book was described in a review as 'an allegory about how to greet the end with grace, how to prepare for your own extinction.') Similarly, in a 'By the Book' interview in *The New York Times*, the novelist Sigrid Nunez illuminated another path for writers to take when she made the following observation: 'Joy Williams once suggested that perhaps it has been a mistake for writers to be focused so obsessively on humans ... I'd like to see more writing about the earth and about non-human beings. I'd like more animals to appear as characters in fiction, but by this I don't mean narratives from an animal's point of view, which I rarely find convincing.'

With the above considerations in mind, here is a list of both fiction and non-fiction that I will choose from for my course:

John Berger, *Hold Everything Dear*
Octavia E. Butler, *The Parable of the Sower*
Rachel Carson, *Silent Spring*
J.M. Coetzee, *Life and Times of Michael K.*

Peter Frankopan, *The Earth Transformed*
Amitav Ghosh, *The Hungry Tide*
Jeff Goodell, *The Heat Will Kill You First*
Katie Holden, ed., *The Language of Trees*
Bohumil Hrabal, *All My Cats*
Dale Jamieson, *Reason in a Dark Time*
Robin Wall Kimmerer, *Braiding Sweetgrass*
Elizabeth Kolbert, *The Sixth Extinction*
Ursula Le Guin, *The Word for World Is Forest*
Lydia Millet, *A Children's Bible*
Sigrid Nunez, *The Friend*
Jenny Offill, *Weather*
Chen Qiufan, *The Waste Tide*
Emily Raboteau, *Lessons for Survival*
Kim Stanley Robinson, *The Ministry for the Future*
Arundhati Roy, *The Cost of Living*
Rebecca Solnit, *Not Too Late*
Greta Thunberg, *No One Is Too Small to Make a Difference*
John Vaillant, *Fire Weather*
Jesmyn Ward, *Salvage the Bones*
David Wallace-Wells, *The Uninhabitable Earth*
Joy Williams, *Ill Nature*

Overleaf:
October, 2022

In the pause between the fire and the flood, Delhi, 2023

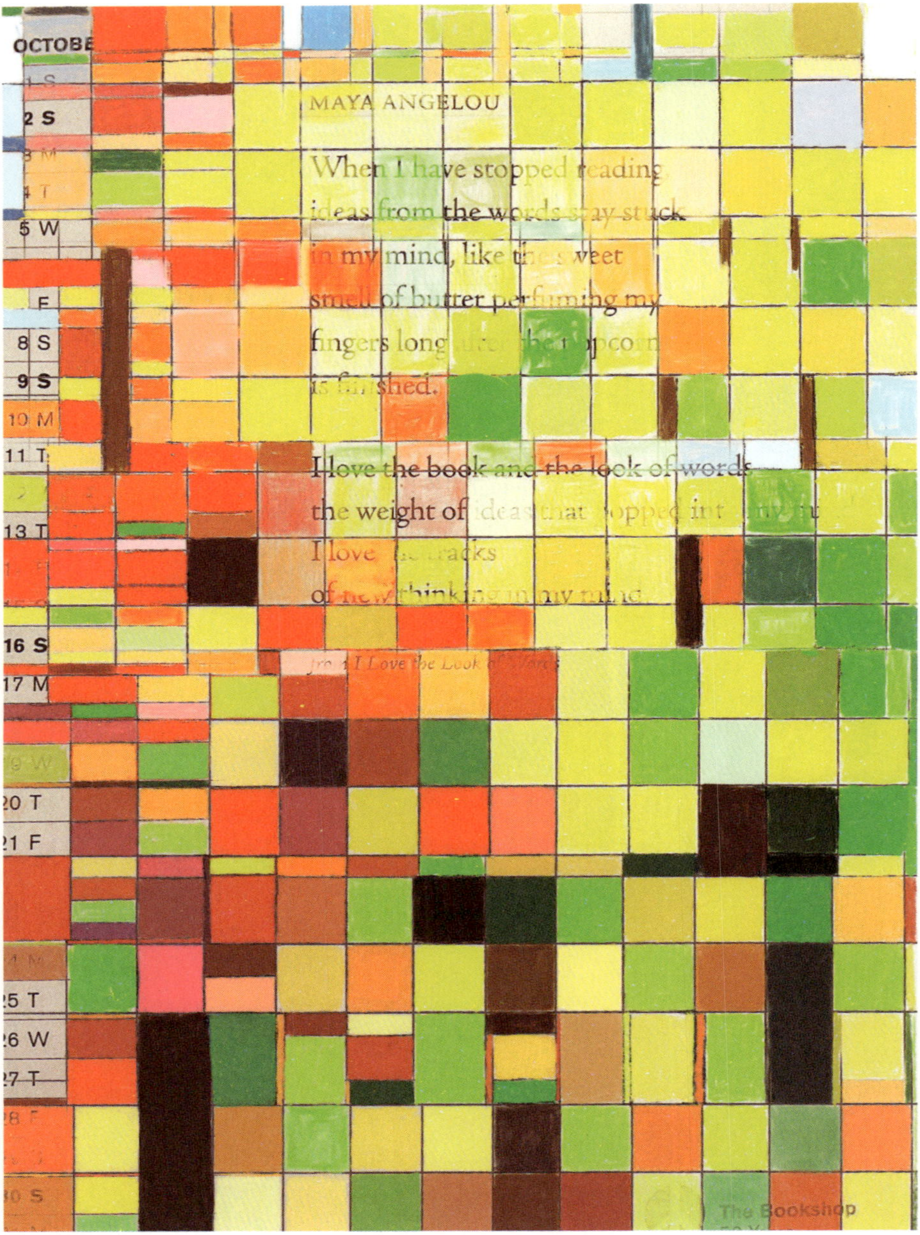
MAYA ANGELOU
When I have stopped reading
ideas from the words stay stuck
in my mind, like the sweet
smell of butter perfuming my
fingers long after the popcorn
is finished.
I love the book and the look of words
the weight of ideas that popped into my mind
I love the tracks
of new thinking in my mind.
from I Love the Look of Words
OCTOBE
2 S
5 W
8 S
9 S
10 M
11 T
13 T
16 S
17 M
20 T
21 F
25 T
26 W
27 T
30 S
The Bookshop

The wind tries to blow the hat away, I wish to keep it on. Amitava, as always, wants to catch what happens in between. fleeting, falling. July 9, 2023, it rained 150 plus mm in the city today. Raj Kamal Jha

Don't Stop Walking

During an interview with David Remnick for *The New Yorker* magazine in 2023, Salman Rushdie said about his writing practice, 'I've got nothing else to do ... I always envied writers like Günter Grass, who had a second career as a visual artist. I thought how nice it must be to spend a day wrestling with words, and then get up and walk down the street to your art studio and become something completely else. I don't have that.' He went on to say: 'When I have a book in my head, it's as if the rest of the world is in its correct shape.' That is a wonderful credo to adopt as a writer; it expresses a fundamental commitment to the act of writing as an organizing principle of one's existence in the world. But I confess I was self-interestedly drawn more to the remarks Rushdie had made about being a visual artist. My drawing practice isn't very old, I've been painting for only a few years, but what I had taken from Rushdie's words was the sense that I was doing the right thing. So often in the past months I had found not just a release but also, on occasion, a new direction in my writing when I had gone away to complete a painting. I also felt happy when I read Rushdie's interview because in my new novel, *My Beloved Life*, it so happened that my co-protagonist Jugnu, as a young reporter in Patna, had written to Günter Grass—and received a response from the famous writer accompanied by one of his drawings of little children in Bengal taking shelter in the rain under a banana leaf.

Opposite: On a walk with Mona, 2023

It is crucial for me that I mix different forms and produce work that defies conventional categories. I had sent Zadie Smith a copy of *The Blue Book*, and then, writing about my time in London, I had put Zadie's words in *The Yellow Book*—but what I want to tell you is that when the latter reached her she wrote to tell me: 'I loved your blue book so much. Am just starting your yellow. Definitions belong to the definers, not the defined is a Toni Morrison quote I feel like typing out to you right now.' But having shared the above, in the spirit of keeping a journal, I cannot resist sharing Zadie's response to reading *The Yellow Book*, a response that admits the possibility of my again quoting her: 'almost finished yr yellow book so know i am at risk of appearing in a sequel but must tell you i read most of it on a plane with my daughter locked in terrible argument and resorting to your book every hour or so like i did with books when I was a child and it was my parents tearing strips off each other—that is, in real need. and every time your book came with something that helped or distracted or soothed or provided beauty. whenever i read in this state of desperation i think its wrong to sneer at the digital realm (as i sometimes do) because i know so exactly the feeling of wanting to escape the present, the desire to be mediated—i was raised that way. the medium changes but the need doesn't.'

I'm committed to writing every day. I'm also an advocate of walking every day. The mantra I offer my students is that each day they write 150 words and walk mindfully for at least ten minutes. In his recent memoir, *Every Man for Himself and God Against All*, Werner Herzog writes that 'the world reveals itself to those who travel on foot'. And: '... again and again (and again), the significance of the world is derived from tiny details never otherwise noted; this is the stuff from which the world may replenish itself. At the end of a day of walking, the wealth of a single day is past counting. When you walk, there is nothing between the lines; everything is in the most immediate and rabid presence.' Many, if not most, of the drawings and paintings in this book are the result of the walks I have undertaken. Don't stop walking! And keep a journal. What you draw is a way of keeping a diary, of course, but also write words to record what you see. 'Pay attention,' instructed Susan Sontag. 'It's all about paying attention. Attention is vitality. It connects you with others. It makes you eager. Stay eager.'

Every now and then there appears on my social media feed, a quote or two about the benefits of keeping a journal. The most persuasive, in my opinion, is the one provided by a character in *The Importance of Being Earnest* by Oscar Wilde: 'I never travel without my diary. One should always have something sensational to read on the train.'

Peonies in Millbrook, 2023

Opposite page:
Sunset Lake, Vassar College, 2023
Hiking near the Shawangunks, 2024

This page:
St. Louis, Missouri, 2024
Before the wall near the Hudson, New York City, 2024

Central Park in March, 2024

Central Park in April, 2024

Central Park in May, 2024

Rock, flower, woman, Central Park, 2024

Forsythia, 2023

Porch rhododendrons, 2023

Outside Sam's studio, 2023

Morning, Poughkeepsie, 2023

Evening, Poughkeepsie, 2023

Bathers, Rishikesh, 2023

That Was January, This Is June

'Happiness? Is there such a thing that you can put your finger on, and be able to say, this is happiness, this is fulfilment?' This question is posed by the Hindi writer Nirmal Verma in a short story titled *'Zindagi Yahan Aur Wahan'*. (The translation is mine. The title of Verma's story has been translated by Vineet Gill as 'Life Here and Thereafter'). Verma goes on to write: '… no, happiness doesn't happen, it exists only as recall—when one is in pain. When you make the sudden discovery, this is June, that was January.' (I like the fact that Verma links misery with the burning heat of June, and happiness with the cold of January, when flowers are in bloom in Delhi's gardens.) We could take this thought in other directions. Example: There is nothing like love; we experience it most poignantly only when we have lost it. The more pressing question that Verma's words evoke in my heart is whether it is always possible to recall life's riches when fate has been particularly miserly.

There's another way to approach this question. Let's look at the drawing I have made here. This was a scene I had witnessed on the banks of the Ganga in Rishikesh. Let me first tell you what you can't see in this piece. In the far distance there were beautiful green mist-covered mountains. And above where I was standing, pilgrims crossed over a suspension bridge as they hurried toward a giant mural of the monkey-god Hanuman on the opposite bank, where, as I was to discover soon, there were temples and ashrams and busy restaurants. Here, in what is represented in the drawing, was the river, the water both cold and quick-flowing. You couldn't stand in the current if you didn't have a secure hold on one of the iron chains that ran down the length of the steps that led to the river. I saw a small group of men (I suspected they were drunk, but I can't be sure) having a lot of fun: They held on to each other and to the metal chain, laughing and dunking their heads in the water. There is one more thing that we don't see in the painting. Only a couple hundred yards downstream, a corpse was being cremated on a pyre around which sat the mourners. The river, and perhaps this river in particular, the mighty Ganga, was the connection between January and June, between the dream of living and the drama of dying. To look at the river, to observe what was happening on its banks, was to experience the indivisibility of existence, its highs and lows.

When I was writing this book, a terrible tragedy occurred in a cherished friend's life: her child, a college student, died by suicide. We live in a terrible world, a cruel world, a world that is utterly unjust, so much death from war and other tragedies. And yet this particular death flung me into dark grief. And it was during this period that I made the above drawing. I was trying to return to the river.

For her part, in a social media post, my friend quoted a haiku by Kobayashi Issa (1763–1828):

This world of dew
is a world of dew
and yet, and yet.

And she added: 'One must believe life is extraordinary.'

So much courage, such faith.

In the face of such resolve, how can I, with my insignificant, lesser sorrows, complain or give up? Not just not give up, what is really demanded of me is that I awake to a sense of wonder. And perhaps that process begins with my recognizing the extraordinary nature of my friend's own words, these words delivered from a place of unfathomable grief. It is important to note here that Kobayashi Issa, who wrote the haiku that my friend had quoted, had himself been familiar with tragedies: his mother died when he was two; his stepmother was cruel to him and he was forced to leave home; he returned to nurse his father through sickness; when he married at fifty-one, a son was born but died within a month; the same happened to a second child, also a son; his third child, a daughter, was born healthy and lived to her first birthday but then, as a result of having contracted smallpox, she too died. The haiku that my friend had quoted is believed to have been written after this child's death. Issa had further sorrows in store. His wife died while giving birth to a fourth child, a son, who also died in infancy because of a nurse's mistake. Issa was paralyzed. He remarried but the marriage ended quickly. After he married for the third time, he suffered the fate of seeing his home burn down. He and his wife were forced to live in a storehouse with no windows. The couple had a child, a daughter, who survived into adulthood—but Issa himself had died even before the baby was born.

And yet, and yet. This was the same Issa who wrote bright lines filled with beauty and laughter. Call it the defiance of spirit, or call it faith, or call it art. For instance, this haiku:

The snow is melting
and the village is flooded
with children.

Snowdrops, 2024

Acknowledgements

Each year, when winter still has its chilly fingers wrapped around us, with snow often hiding the covering of dead leaves in my backyard, the snowdrops appear, pushing tenderly out of cold earth. I'm so grateful to the snowdrops, to the changing seasons, to all the rites of nature, and to everything vital that renews our world.

A friend in London, Shefali Malhoutra, after walking with me in Regent's Park, gave me a book that is an anthology of literary works inspired by that park. The book's title is *Park Notes*. The editor is Sarah Pickstone, an artist, who has accompanied each piece with her drawings. I love parks and I found the book inspiring but what has haunted me ever since I read the book is a line in the essay on the acclaimed writer Stevie Smith. (I'm grateful for her poem 'Not Waving but Drowning'.) Here is the line in question: 'Smith drew small pictures to accompany many of her poems, *which made it more difficult to find publishers at the time*.' I have added emphasis because work that is unconventional or that crosses genres generally runs counter to the desires of the gatekeepers. I bring this up only so that I can once again express my gratitude to Hemali Sodhi from A Suitable Agency for her direction and unflagging support, and, in equal measure, to Udayan Mitra, my editor at HarperCollins India, for his thoughtfulness, encouragement and sharp insight.

I'm grateful to the Dorothy and Lewis B. Cullman Center for Scholars and Writers at the New York Public Library where I was the Mary Ellen von der Heyden Fellow during 2023-24. Also to the curators of the Berg Collection, Carolyn Vega and Julie Carlsen, as well as the librarian Rebecca Federman. And to the Yaddo Corporation for a residency during July 2023. I'm thankful to the Research Committee at Vassar College that assisted me with a travel grant. And to Elizabeth Bradley and Bill Hoynes at Vassar College for their support.

No book that is focused on the green planet can turn away from the future; I'm grateful to the young all over the world who are fighting for a more livable planet. I'm grateful to scientists, activists and writers who are trying very hard to educate us. This book is dedicated to my children and to the children of my friends who will not only inherit but also change the future.

Even an apple tree is liable to live for about 100 years, so the Cox I planted in 1936 may still be bearing fruit well into the twenty-first century. An oak or a beech may live for hundreds of years and be a pleasure to thousands or tens of thousands of people before it is finally sawn up into timber. I am not suggesting that one can discharge all one's obligations towards society by means of a private re-afforestation scheme. Still, it might not be a bad idea, every time you commit an antisocial act, to make a note of it in your diary, and then, at the appropriate season, push an acorn into the ground.

— George Orwell

An exercise for those who have finished reading the book.

Choose your own caption:

Caption 1. Devprayag II. (Go back and look at the painting from Devprayag in the chapter 'Postcards from the Ganga'.)

Caption 2. *The Green Book*. (This is the third, and final, book in a trilogy. *The Blue Book* and *The Yellow Book* have now led to *The Green Book*. Hope you have enjoyed all three.)

Author photo: Beowulf Sheehan

AMITAVA KUMAR is the author of several books of fiction and non-fiction. His work has appeared in *Granta*, *The New York Times*, *Harper's*, and several other publications. He has been awarded a Guggenheim fellowship and is currently a Cullman Center Fellow at the New York Library. His novel *Immigrant, Montana* was on the Best of the Year lists at *The New Yorker*, *The New York Times*, and Barack Obama's list of his favourite books of 2018. His 2021 novel *A Time Outside This Time* was described by *The New Yorker* as a 'shimmering assault on the Zeitgeist'. *My Beloved Life*, his latest novel, was published in 2024. *The Blue Book: A Writer's Journal*, and *The Yellow Book: A Traveller's Diary*, published by HarperCollins in 2022 and 2023 respectively, met with a very positive response from readers and critics alike. Kumar is professor of English at Vassar College in upstate New York.

HarperCollins *Publishers* India

At HarperCollins India, we believe in telling the best stories and finding the widest readership for our books in every format possible. We started publishing in 1992; a great deal has changed since then, but what has remained constant is the passion with which our authors write their books, the love with which readers receive them, and the sheer joy and excitement that we as publishers feel in being a part of the publishing process.

Over the years, we've had the pleasure of publishing some of the finest writing from the subcontinent and around the world, including several award-winning titles and some of the biggest bestsellers in India's publishing history. But nothing has meant more to us than the fact that millions of people have read the books we published, and that somewhere, a book of ours might have made a difference.

As we look to the future, we go back to that one word—a word which has been a driving force for us all these years.

Read.